INTRODUCTION:

Welcome to my second collection of photos. I'm the editor and publisher of the *Flash*, the newsletter for the Greater San Antonio Camera Club in San Antonio, Texas. I'm also the club's webmaster. My photos have won several awards in county fairs and camera club competitions. I enjoy photographing architecture and landscapes.

I started looking through my photos and choosing images for a second book after completing my previous photo book, *A Look Through My Lens*. After I put together a list of photos to include in this book, my computer's hard drive crashed. I was able to recover many files, but a couple of photos that I planned to include here were not recoverable. One was a photo of the Texas capitol building taken at night.

One photo that I thought was lost is "Carousel Zebra". I took that photo during a camera club outing. I lost the folder of images from that outing. Fortunately, I had submitted that photo in a camera club competition. I organize the images for the club's digital competitions. I found that I had a copy of that image saved in a folder with other competition entries.

I'm fortunate that I didn't lose much material when my hard drive crashed. After that experience, I bought a backup drive.

I use only digital cameras now, but this book also includes some photos that I took with print and slide film. Please enjoy the images on the pages ahead!

Sincerely,
Adam Kincher

Coast Guard Demonstration

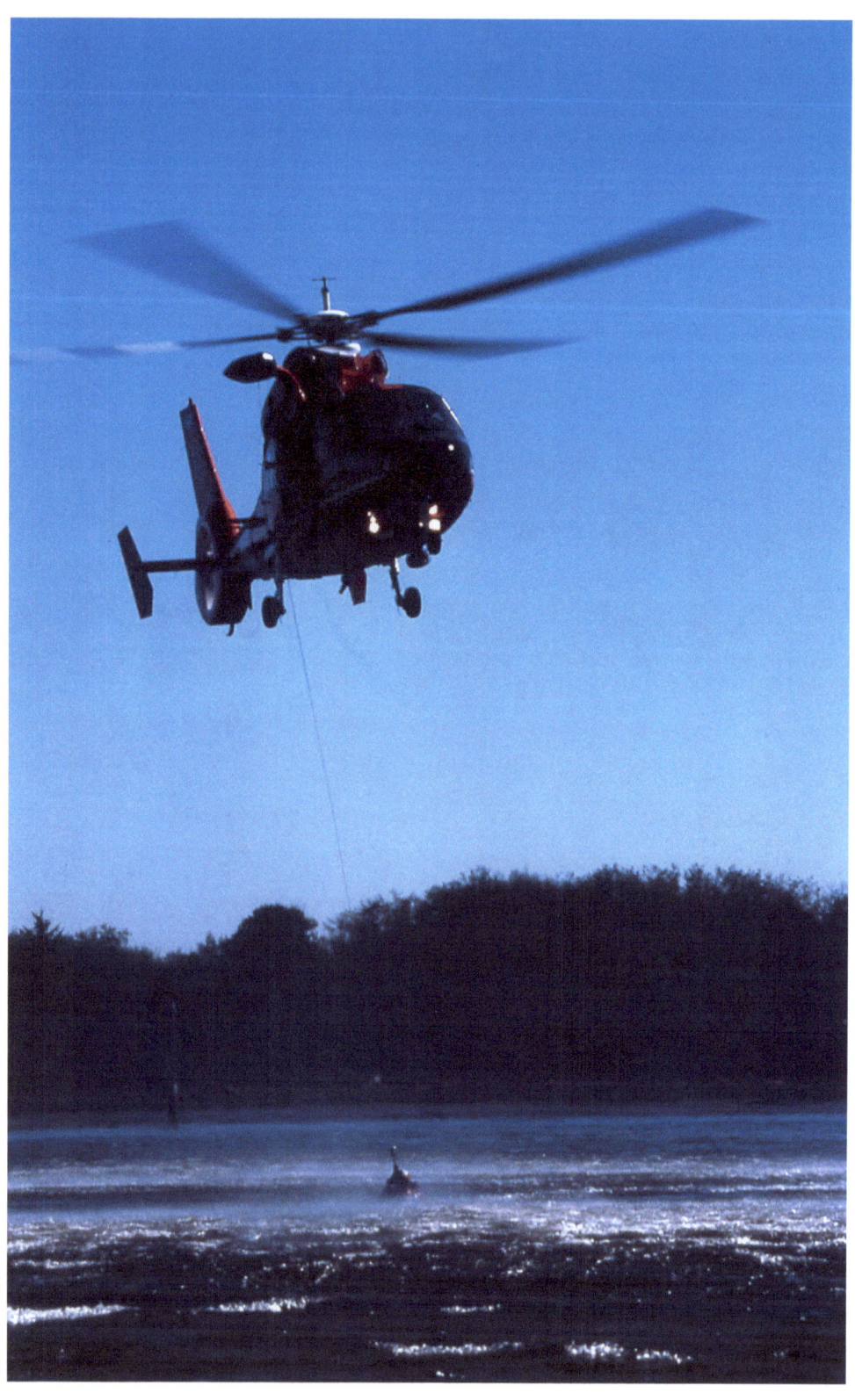

Coast Guard Demonstration in Coos Bay, Oregon

Coast Guard Crew

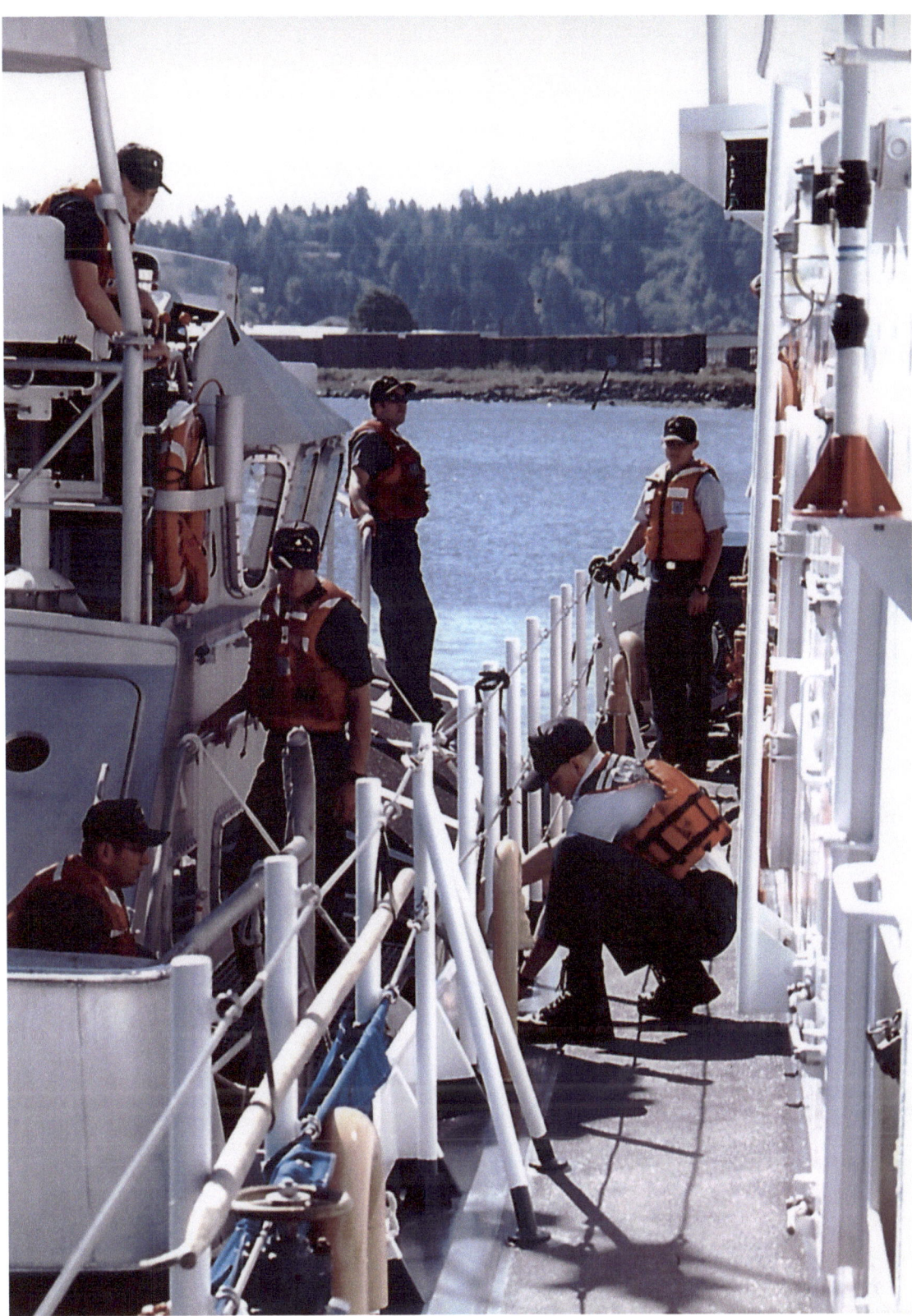

Two Coast Guard ships dock together during a demonstration in Coos Bay, Oregon

Cape Meares Lighthouse

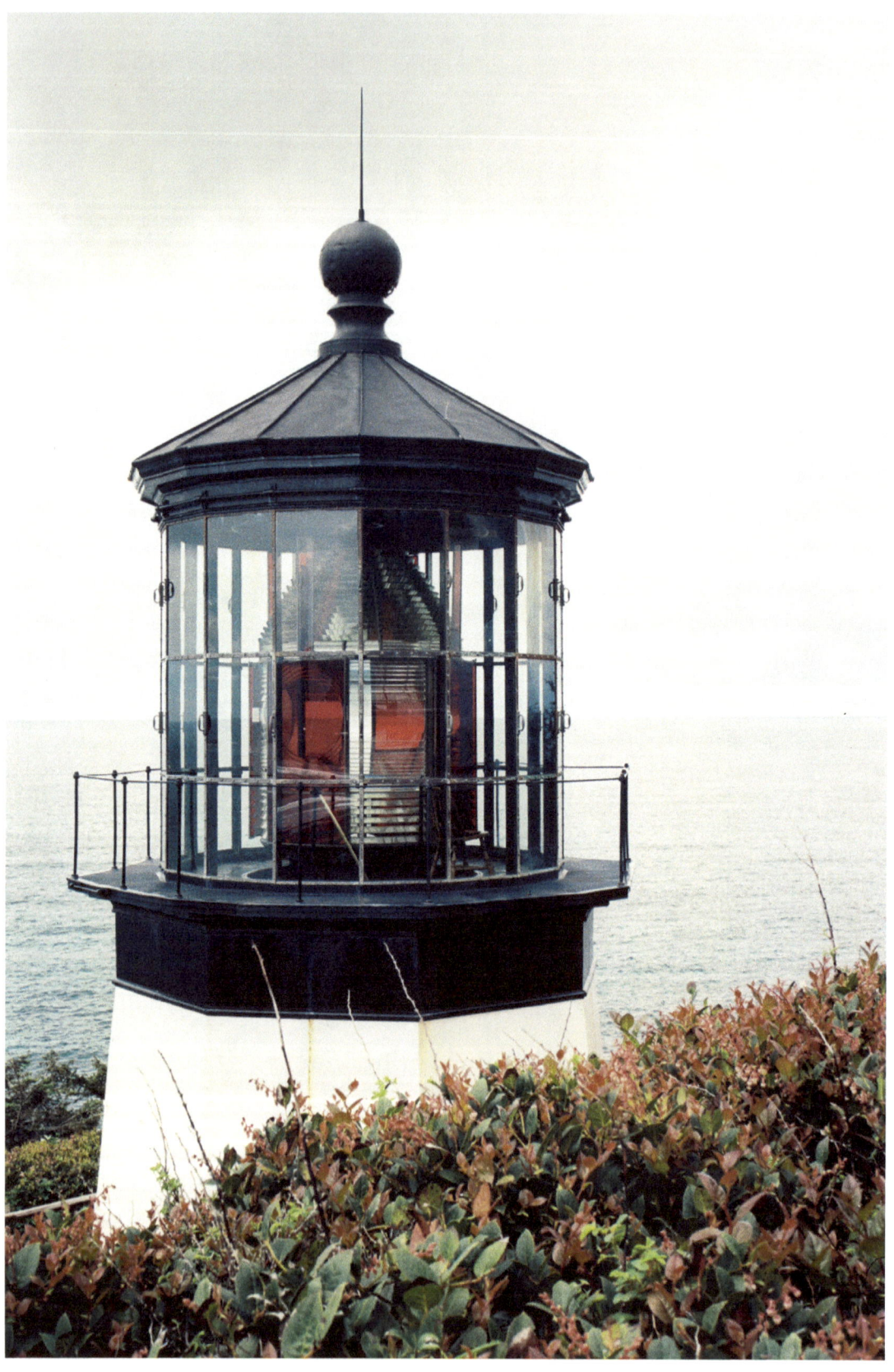

This lighthouse on Oregon's northern coast is the state's shortest lighthouse. There's a great view of the ocean from the tower. Building a tall lighthouse at this location wasn't necessary.

Crater Lake

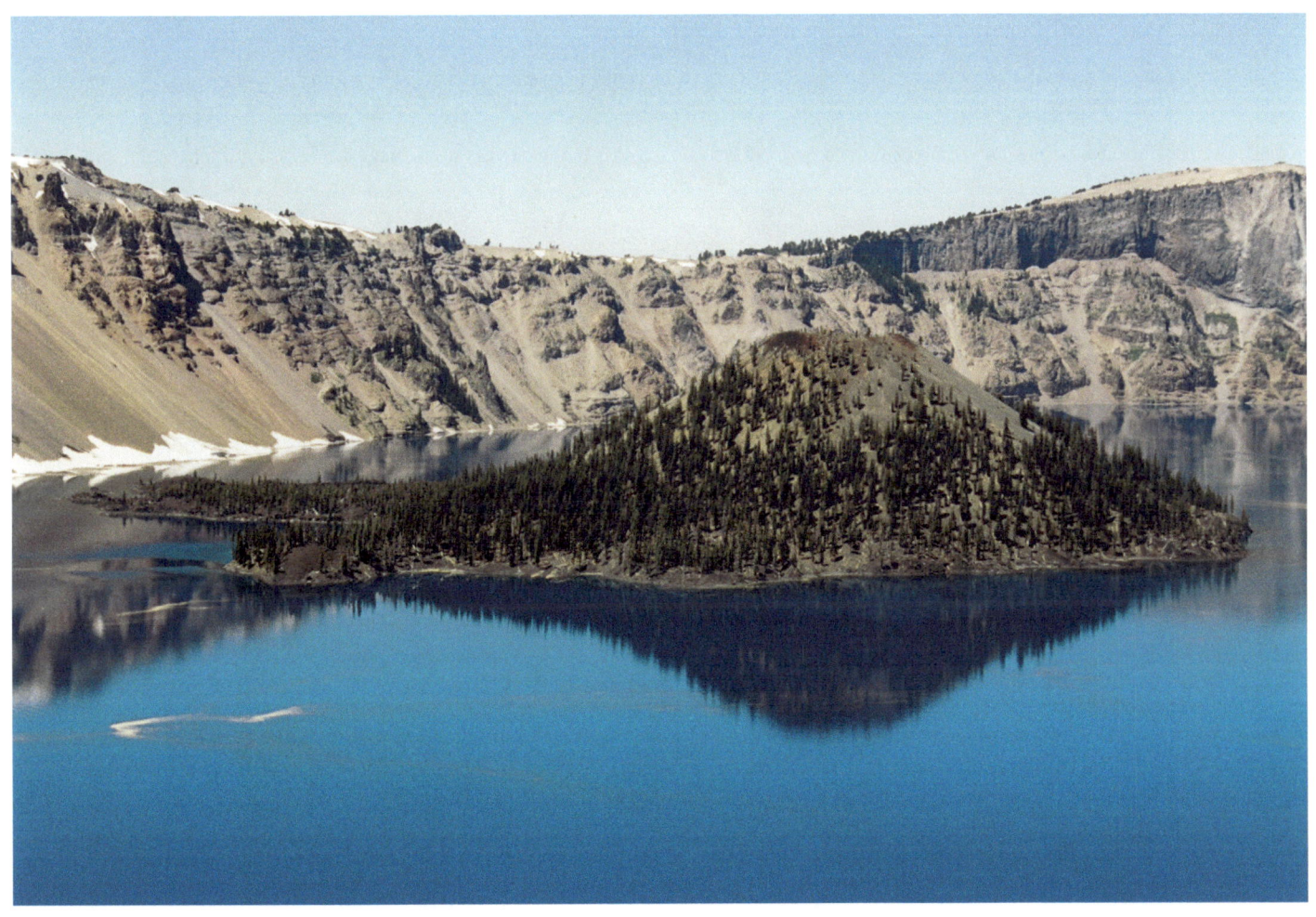

Crater Lake in Oregon on a summer afternoon

Yaquina Head Lighthouse

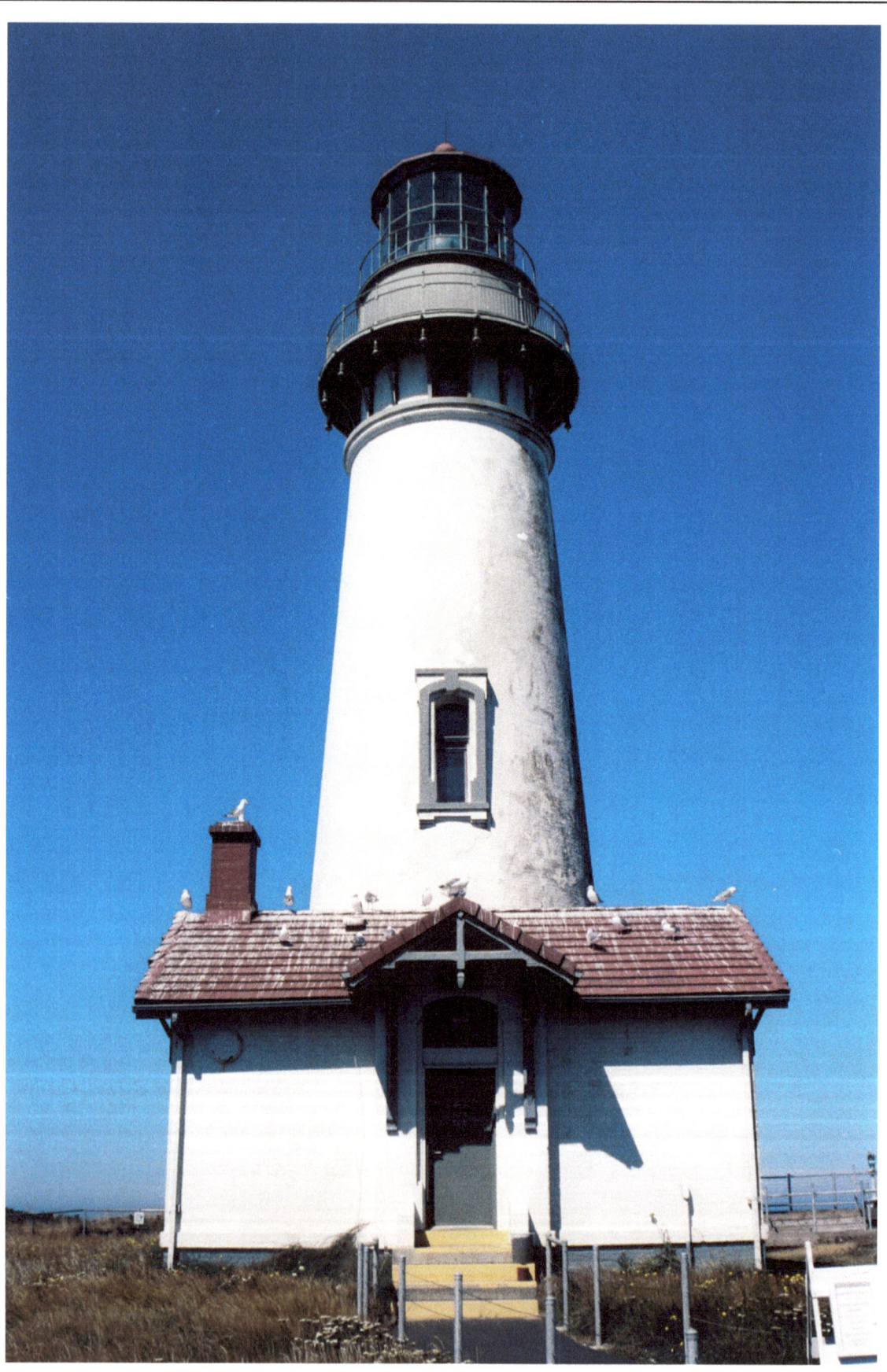

Yaquina Head Lighthouse: Oregon's tallest lighthouse is north of Newport, Oregon.

Bandon Bird

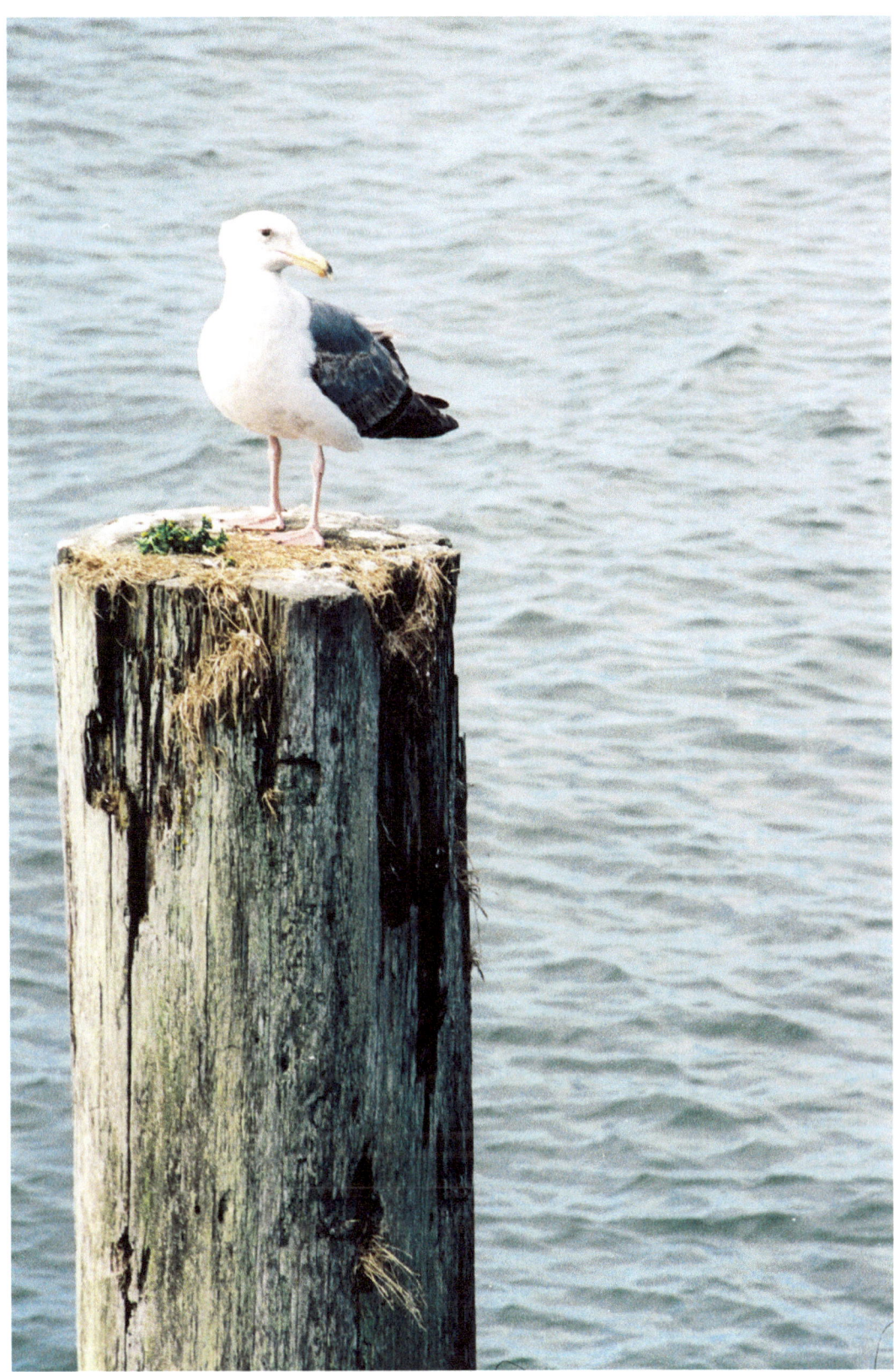

Taken in Bandon, Oregon

Fuel Pump

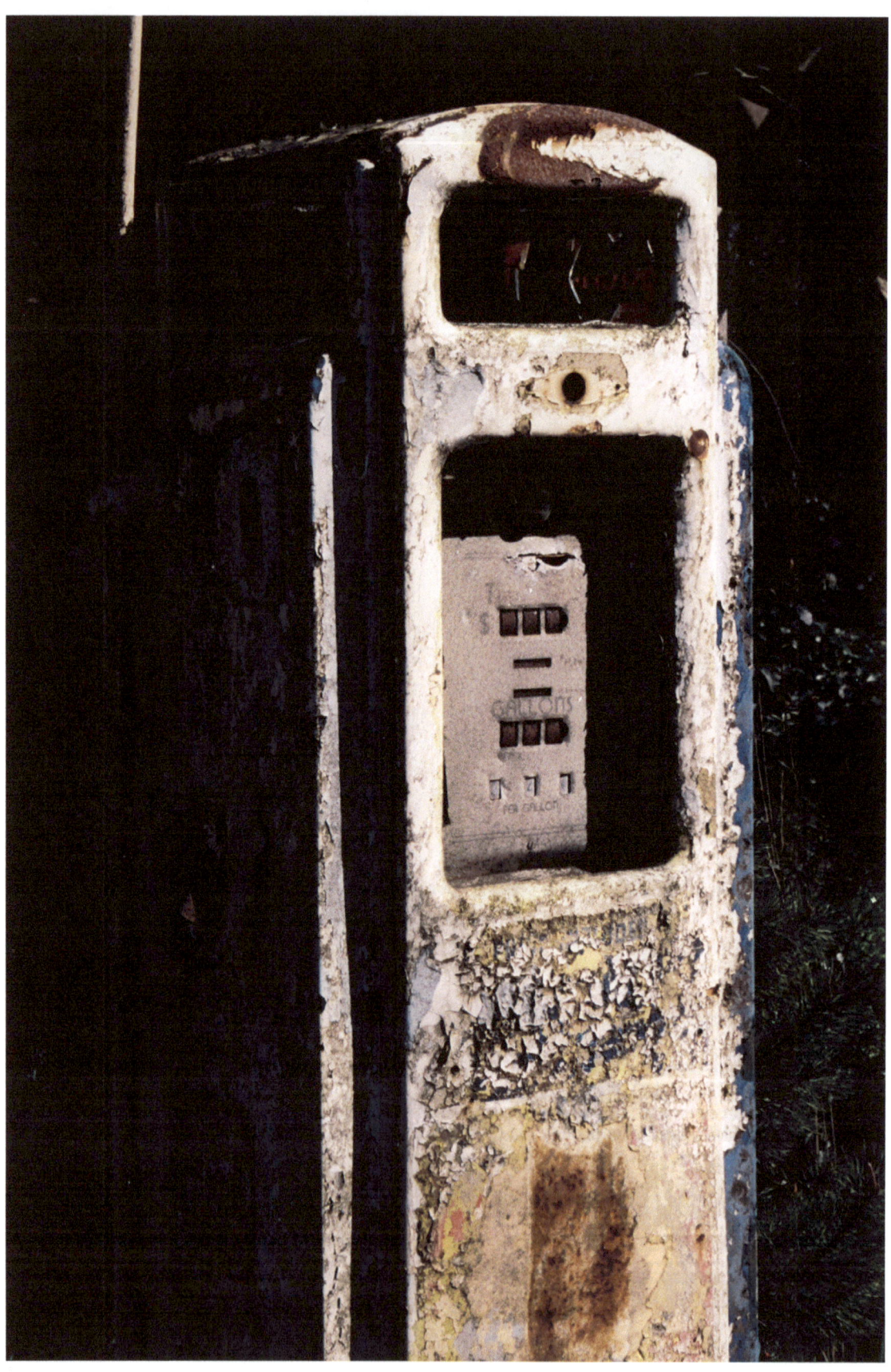

Decaying old fuel pump south of Bandon, Oregon

Heceta Tower

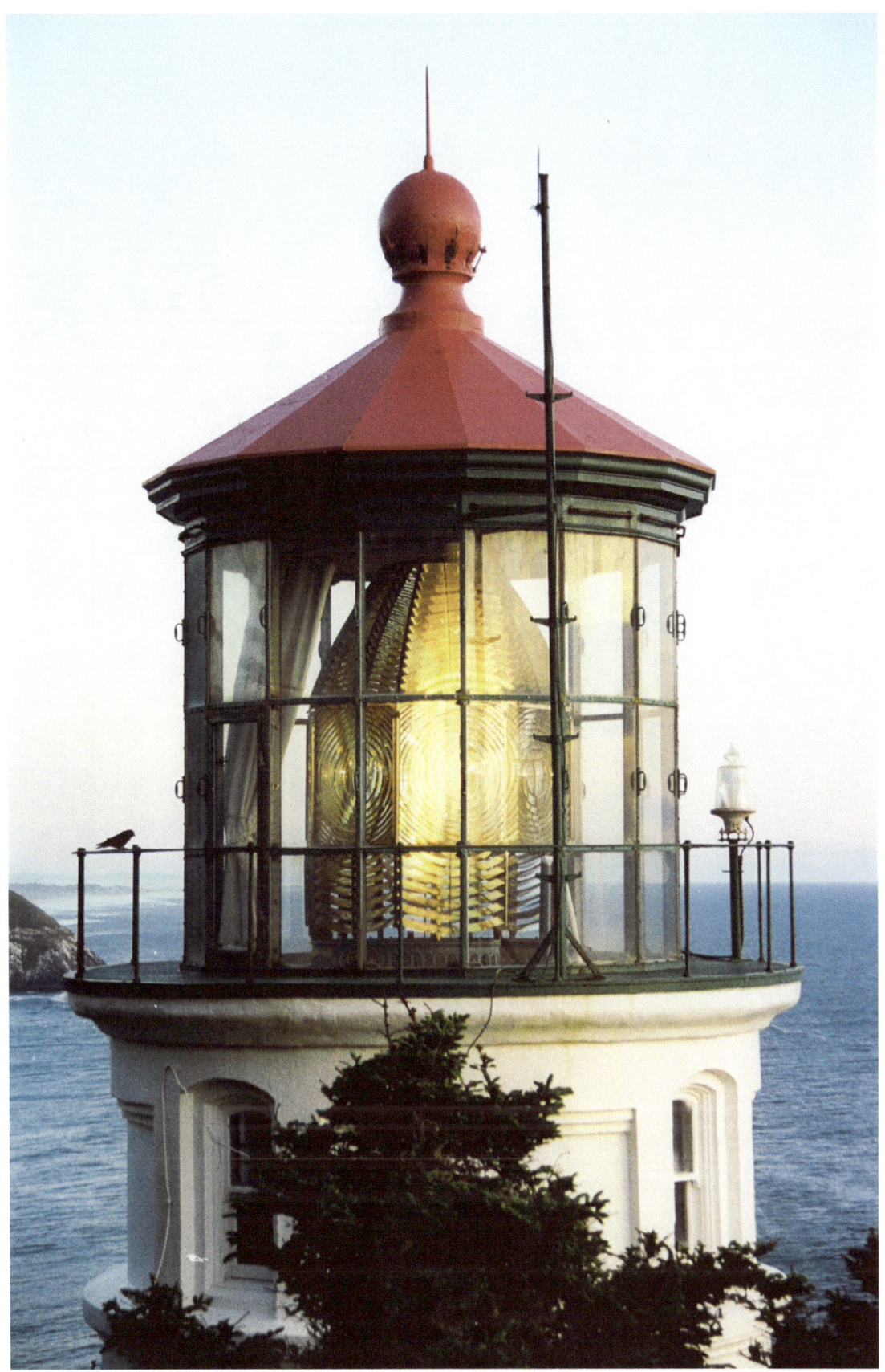

Tower of the Heceta Head Lighthouse north of Florence, Oregon

Moore Mill Truck Shop

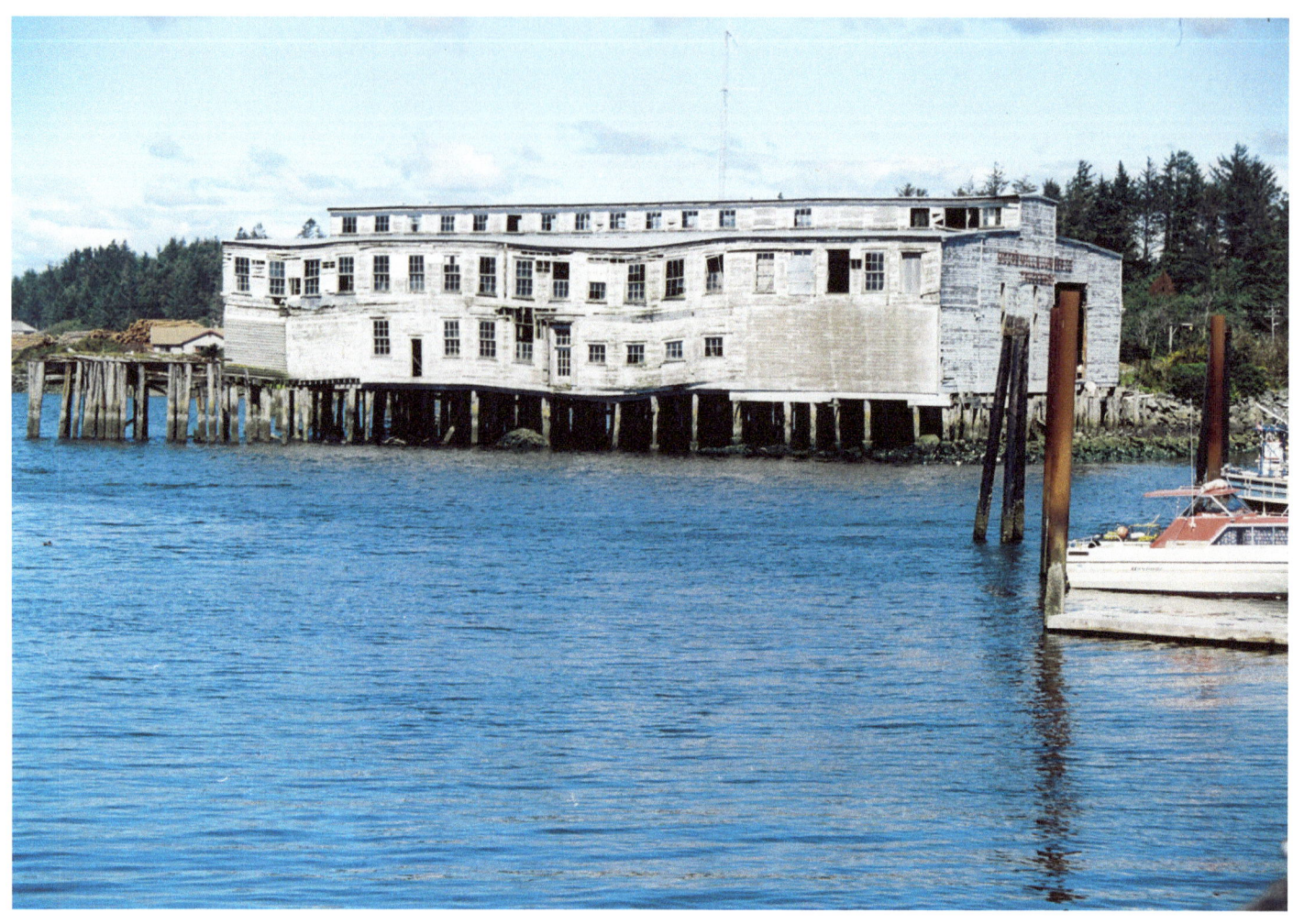

This deteriorating building was a landmark in Bandon, Oregon. The remainder of it was demolished in August 2001.

Capitol Dome

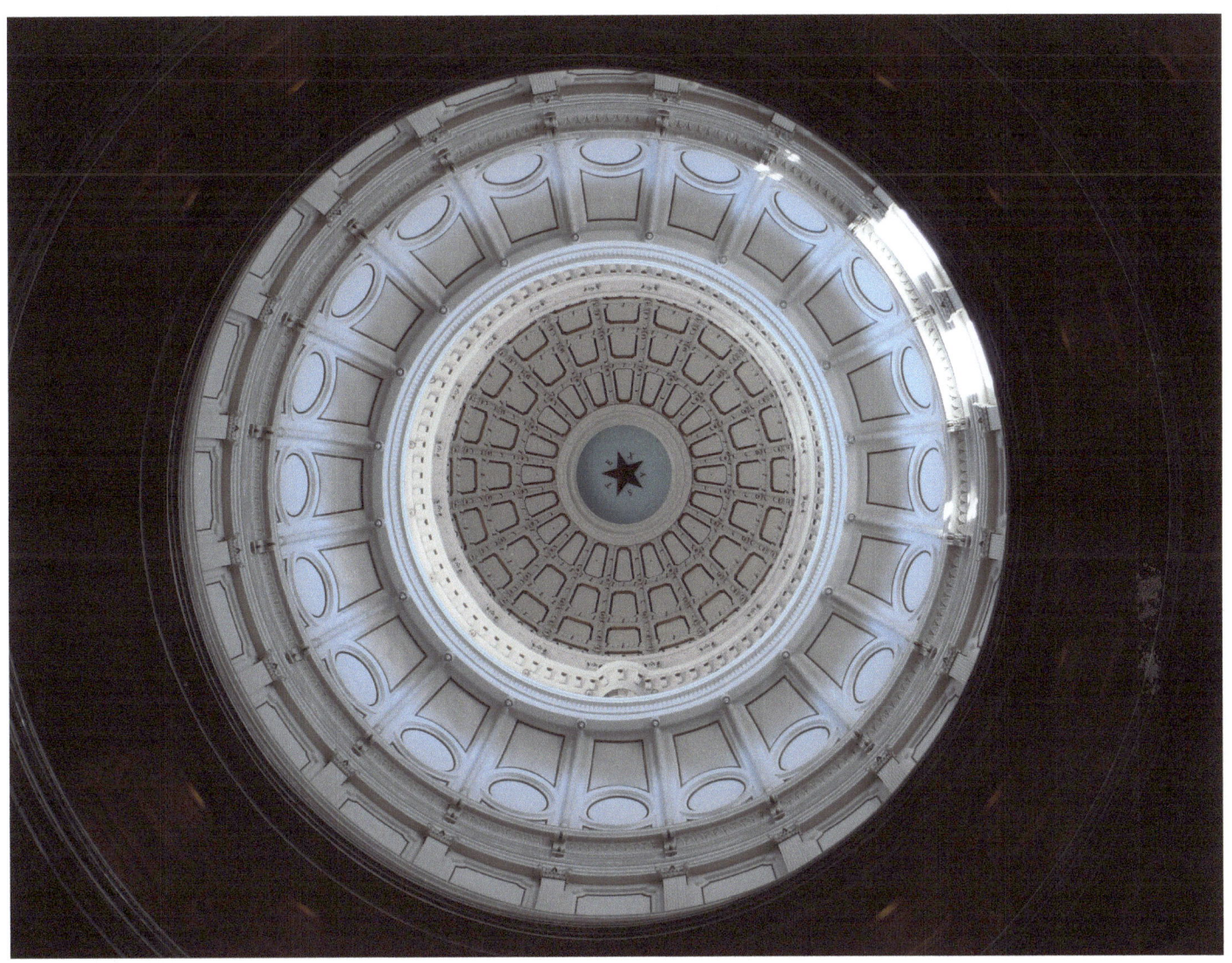

Interior of the dome of the Texas capitol building in Austin, Texas

Russian Plane

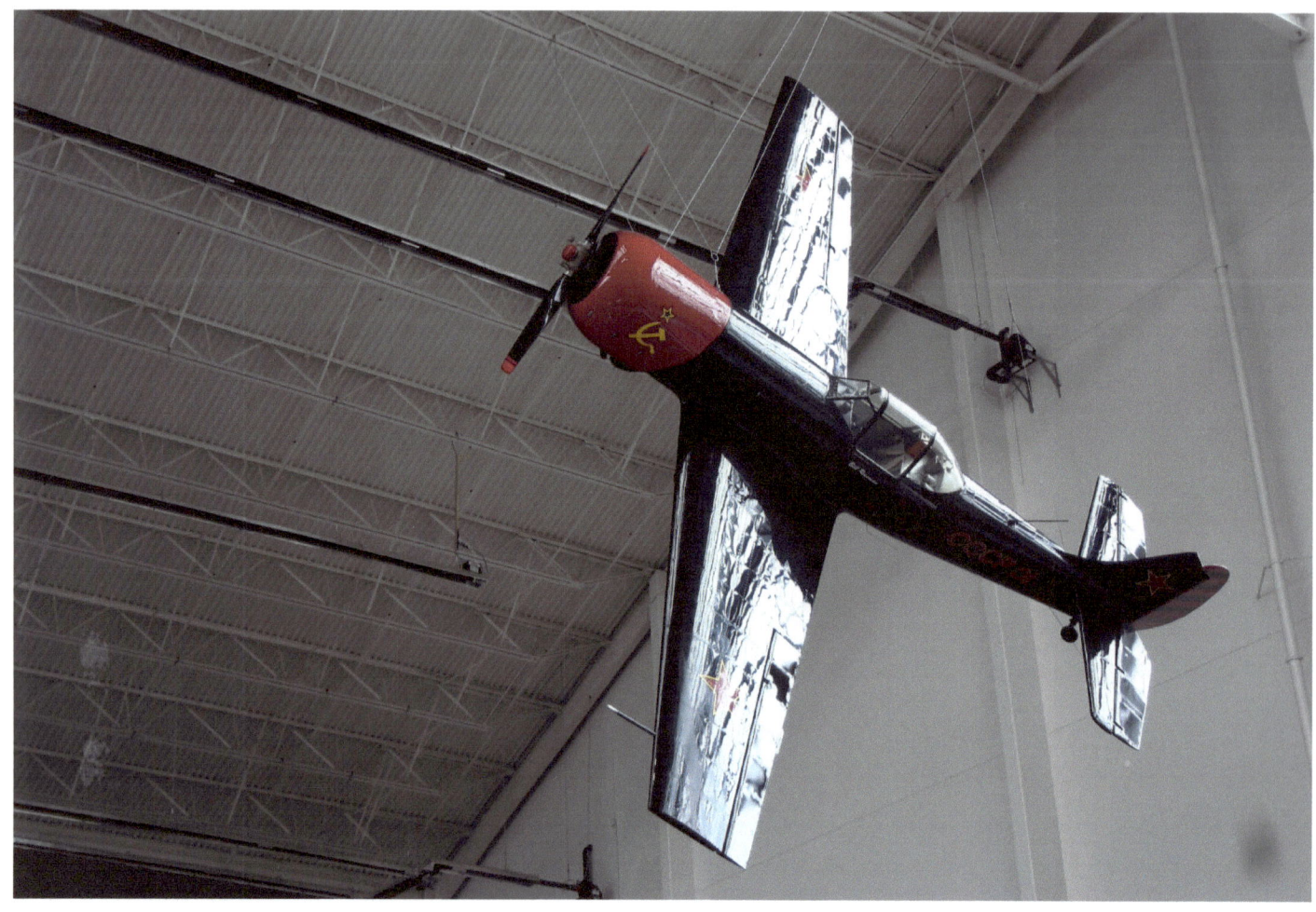

This plane is on display at the Evergreen Aviation and Space Museum in McMinnville, Oregon.

Salem Statue

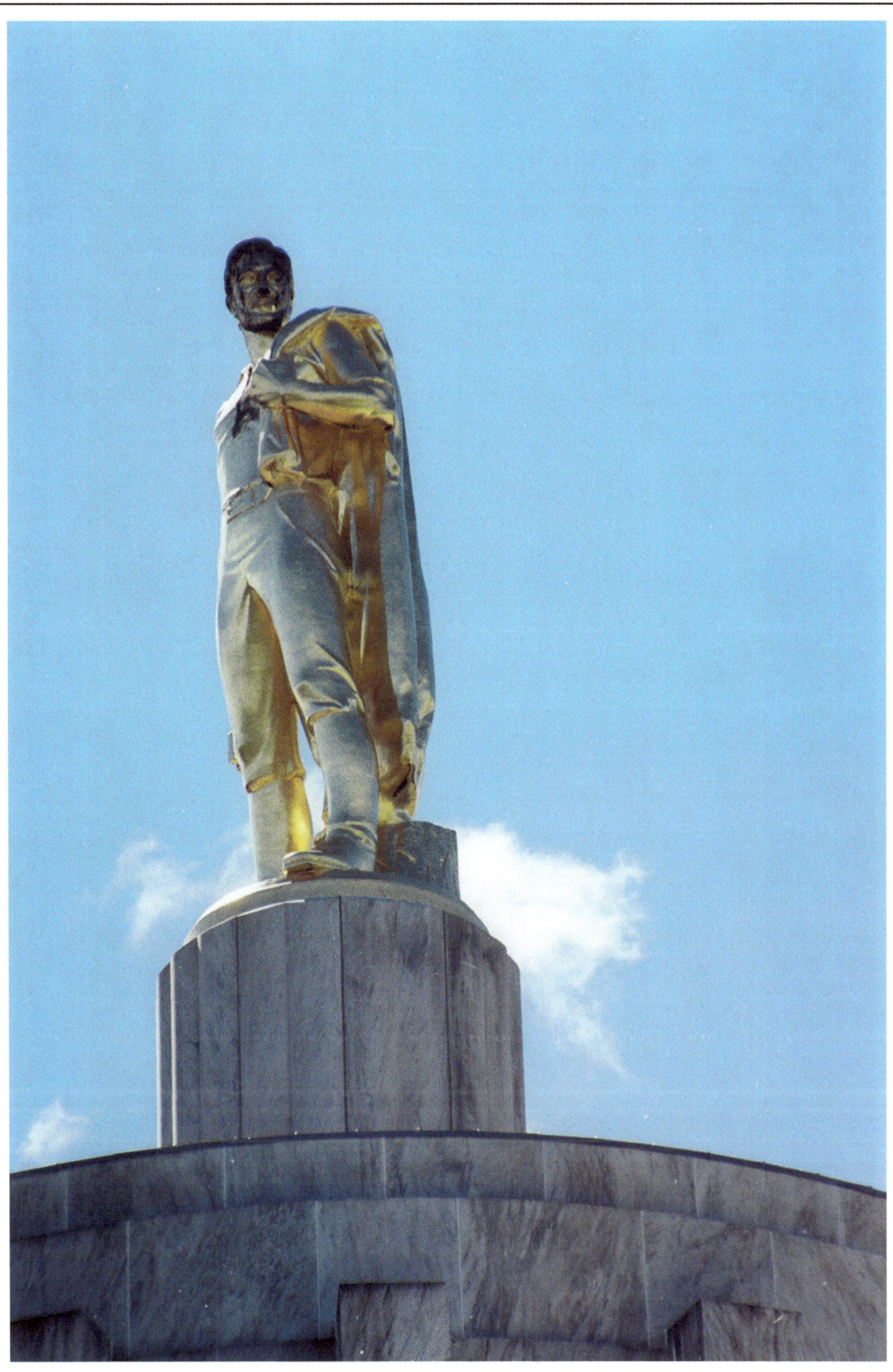

Statue on top of the state capitol building in Salem, Oregon

Silver Falls

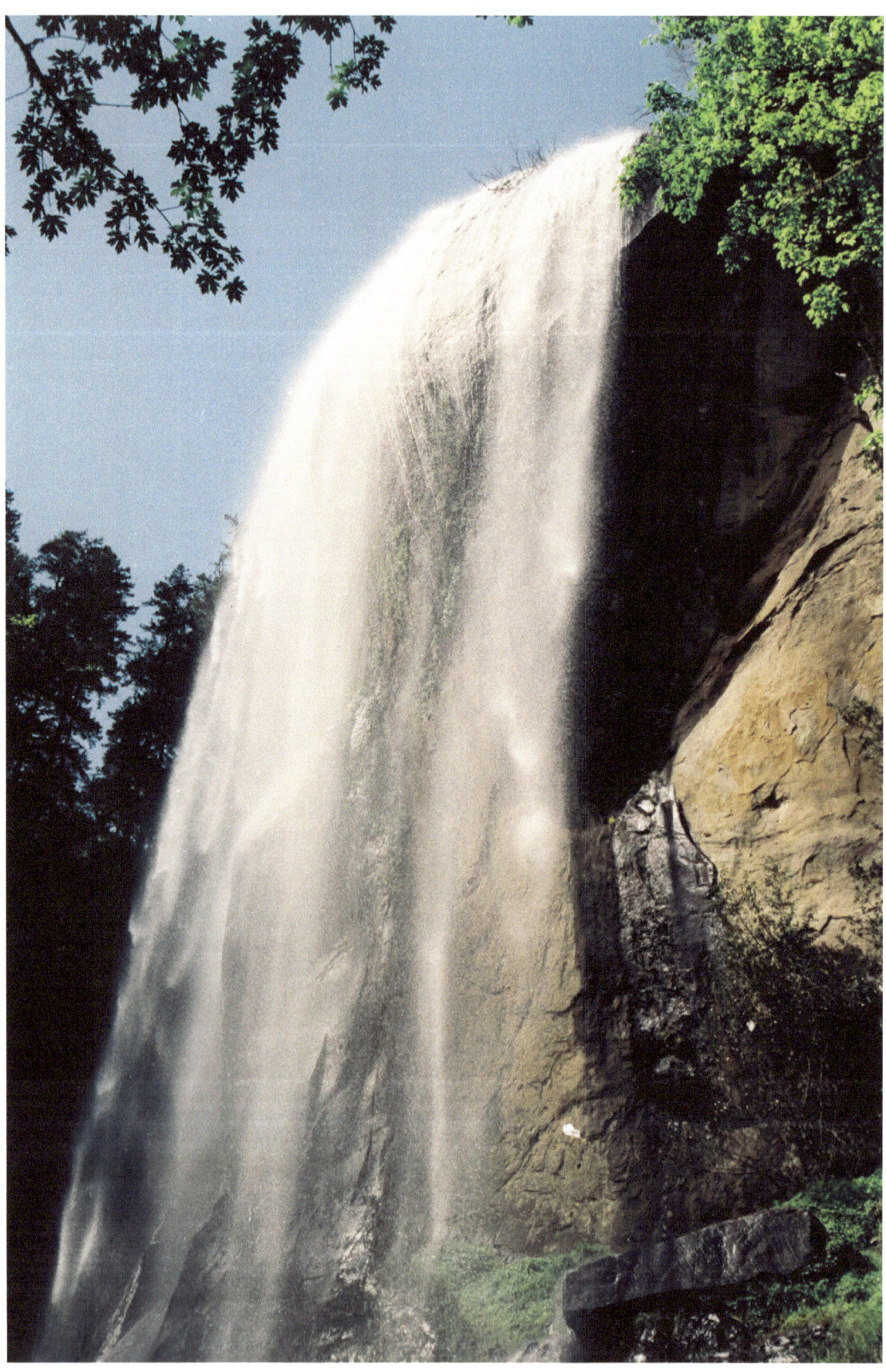

Silver Falls at Golden and Silver Falls State Park near Coos Bay, Oregon

Tulips

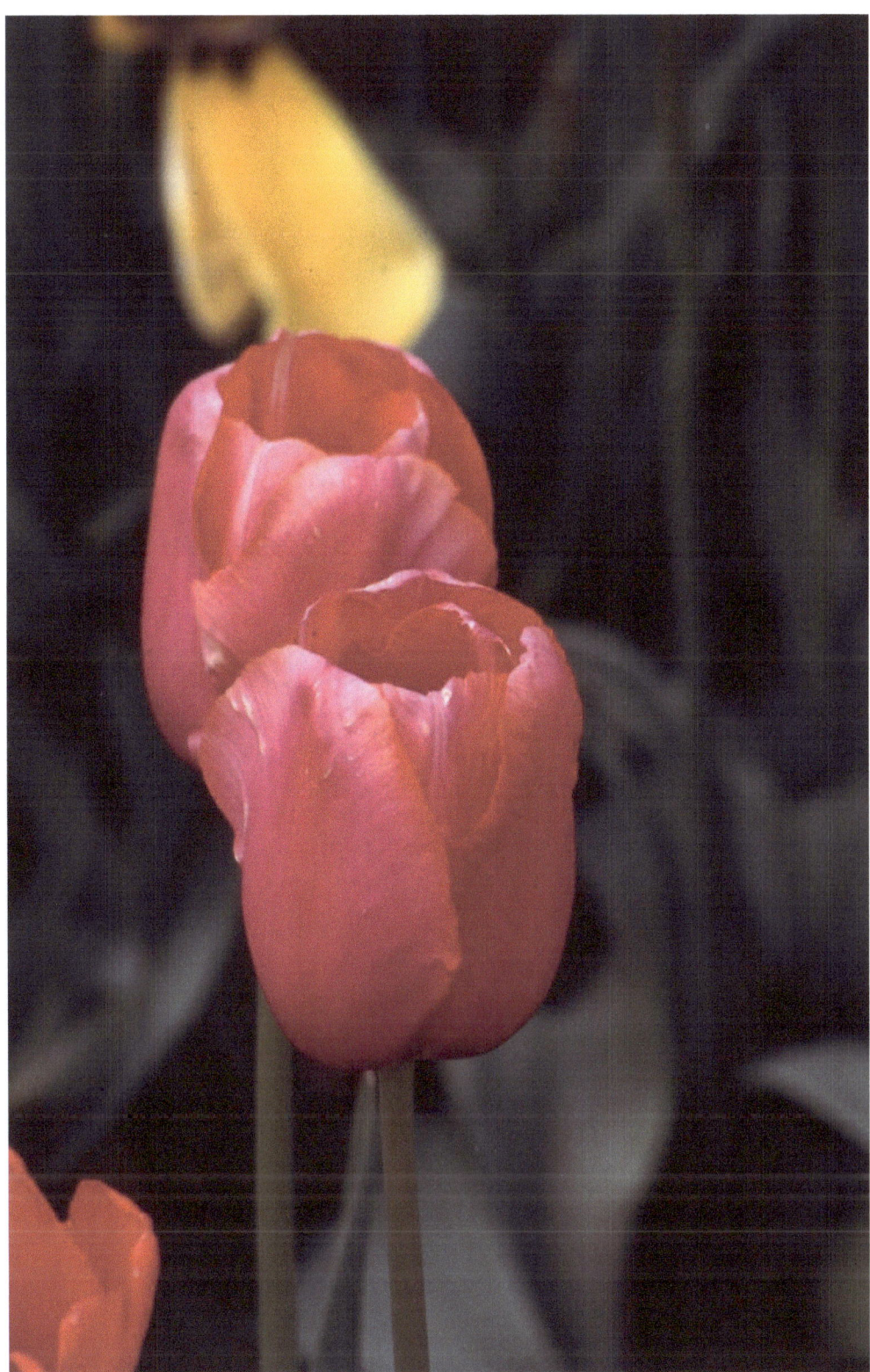

Tulips in Mt. Angel, Oregon

Bike Race

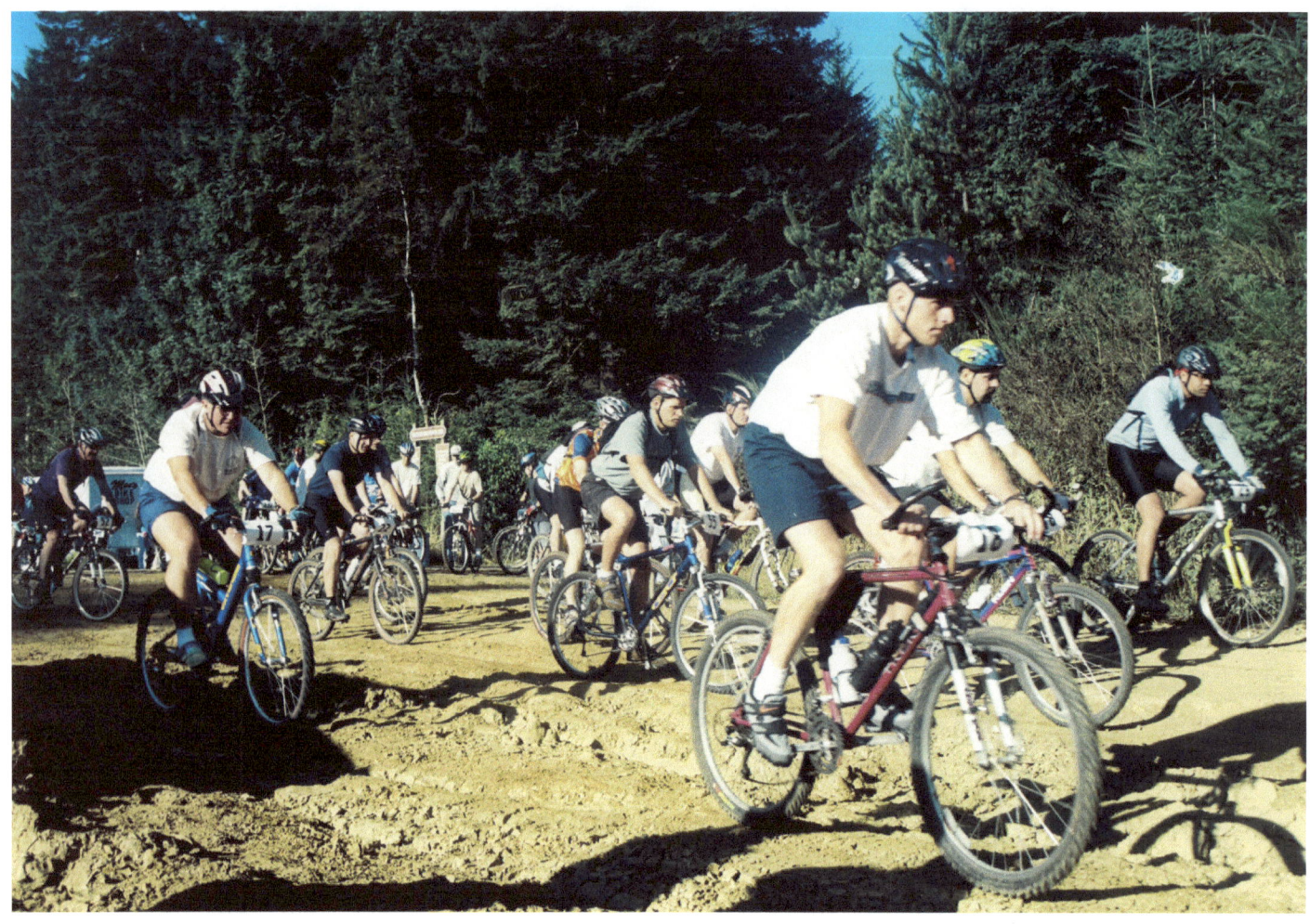

Start of a bike race near Coos Bay, Oregon. This race was one of the activities that took place during the area's annual Bay Area Fun Festival

The Alamo

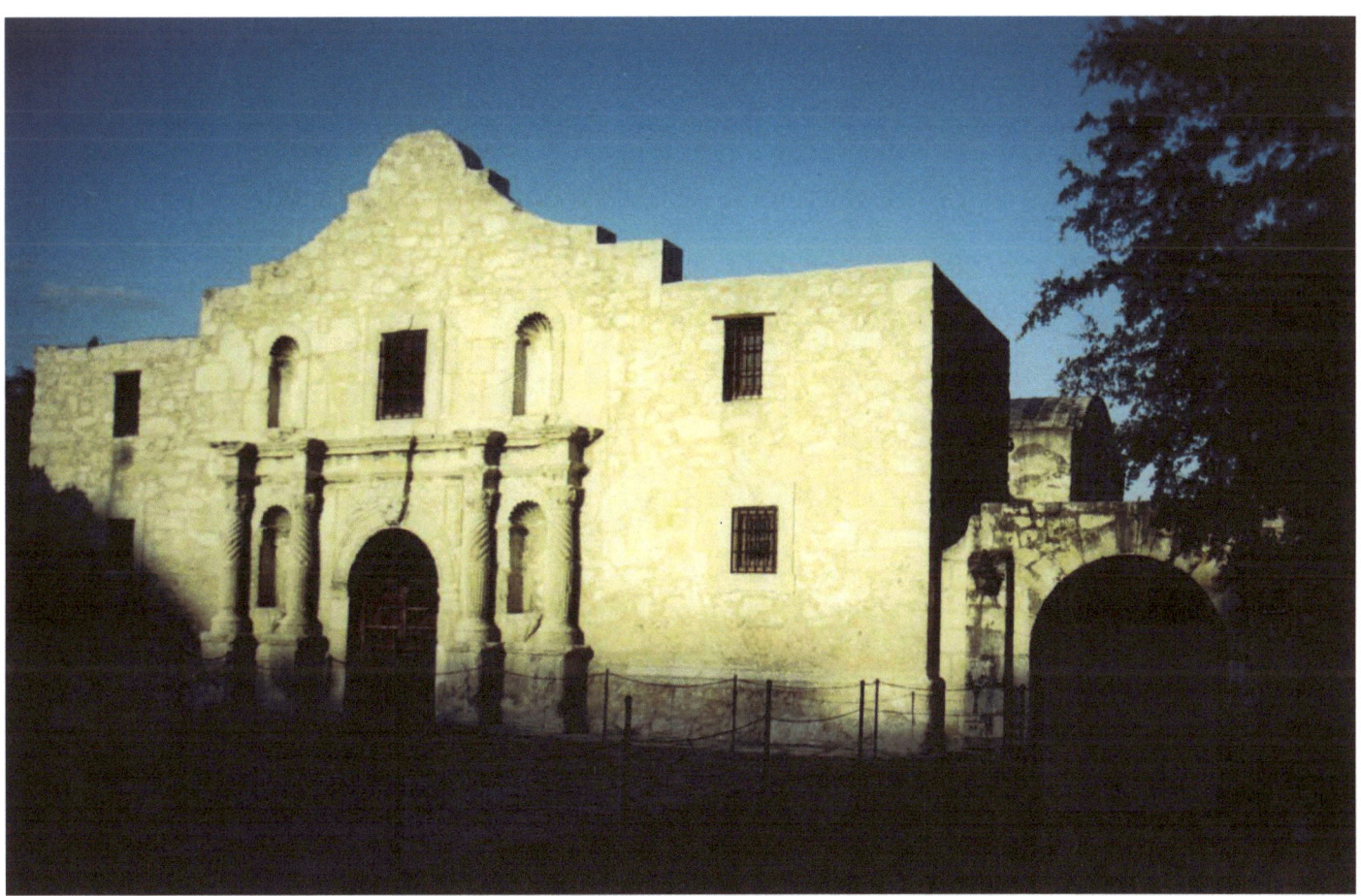

San Antonio, Texas

Reflected Flags

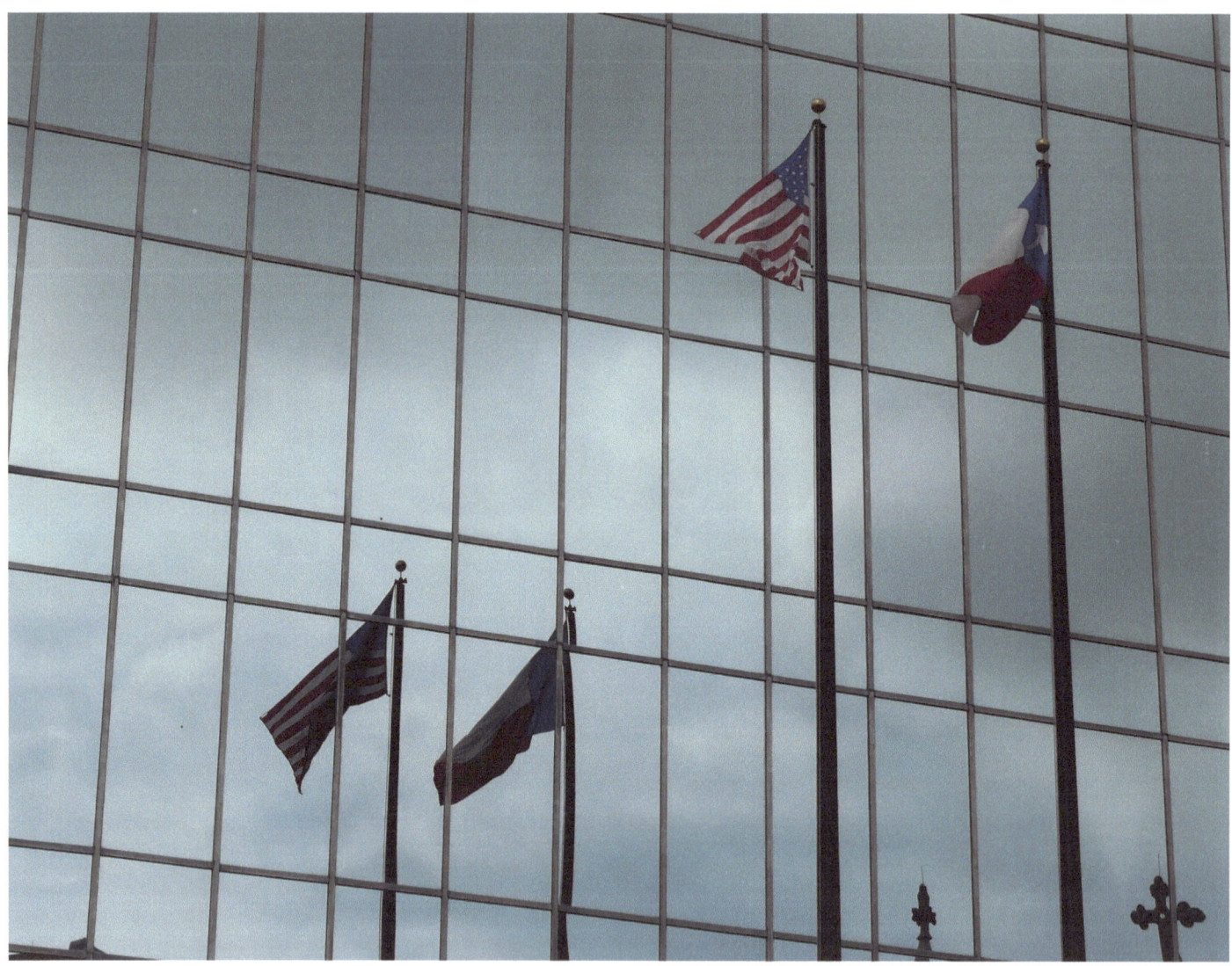

Flags reflected in the windows of a building in Austin, Texas

Johnson County Courthouse

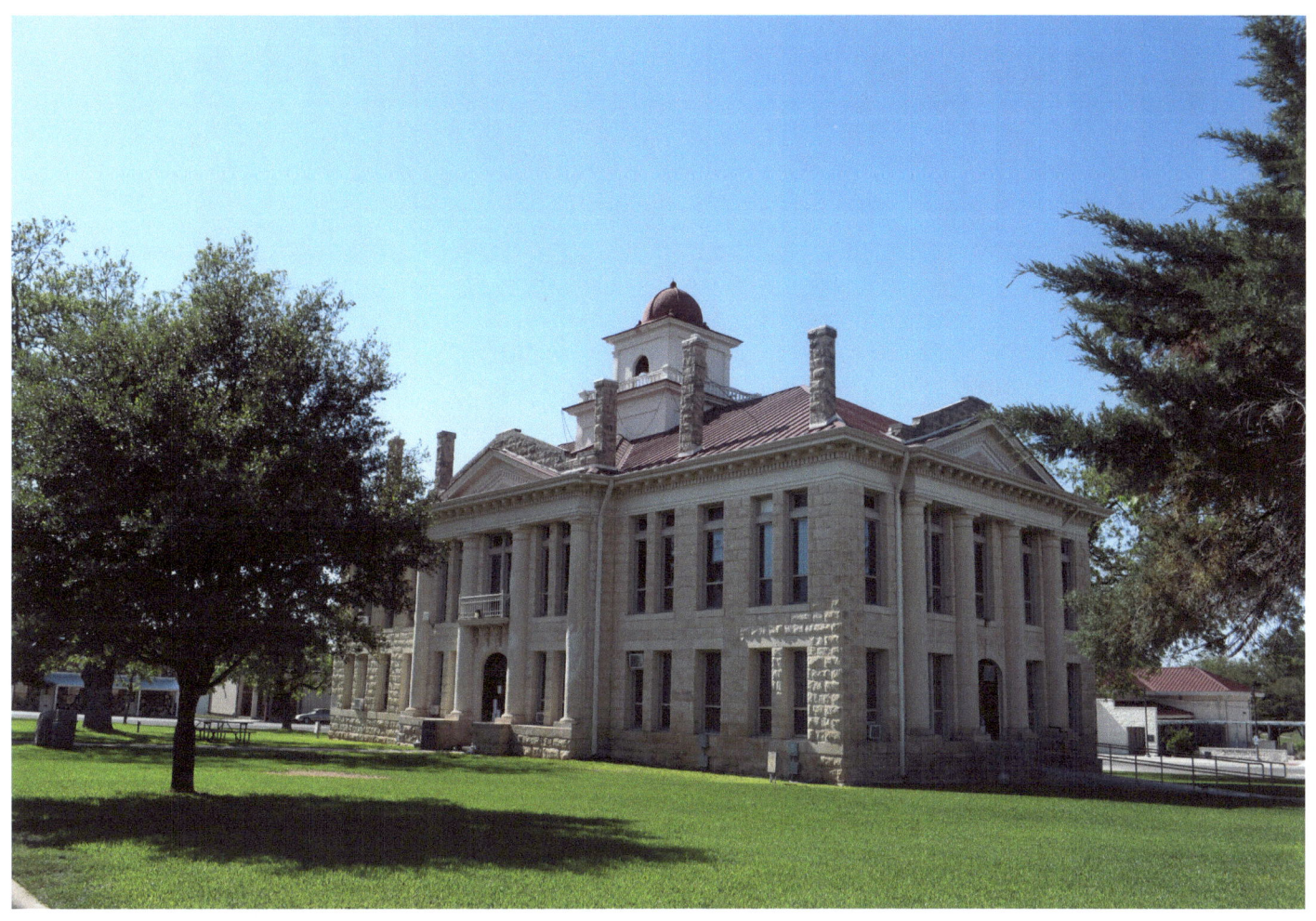

Johnson County Courthouse in Johnson City, Texas

Bluebonnets

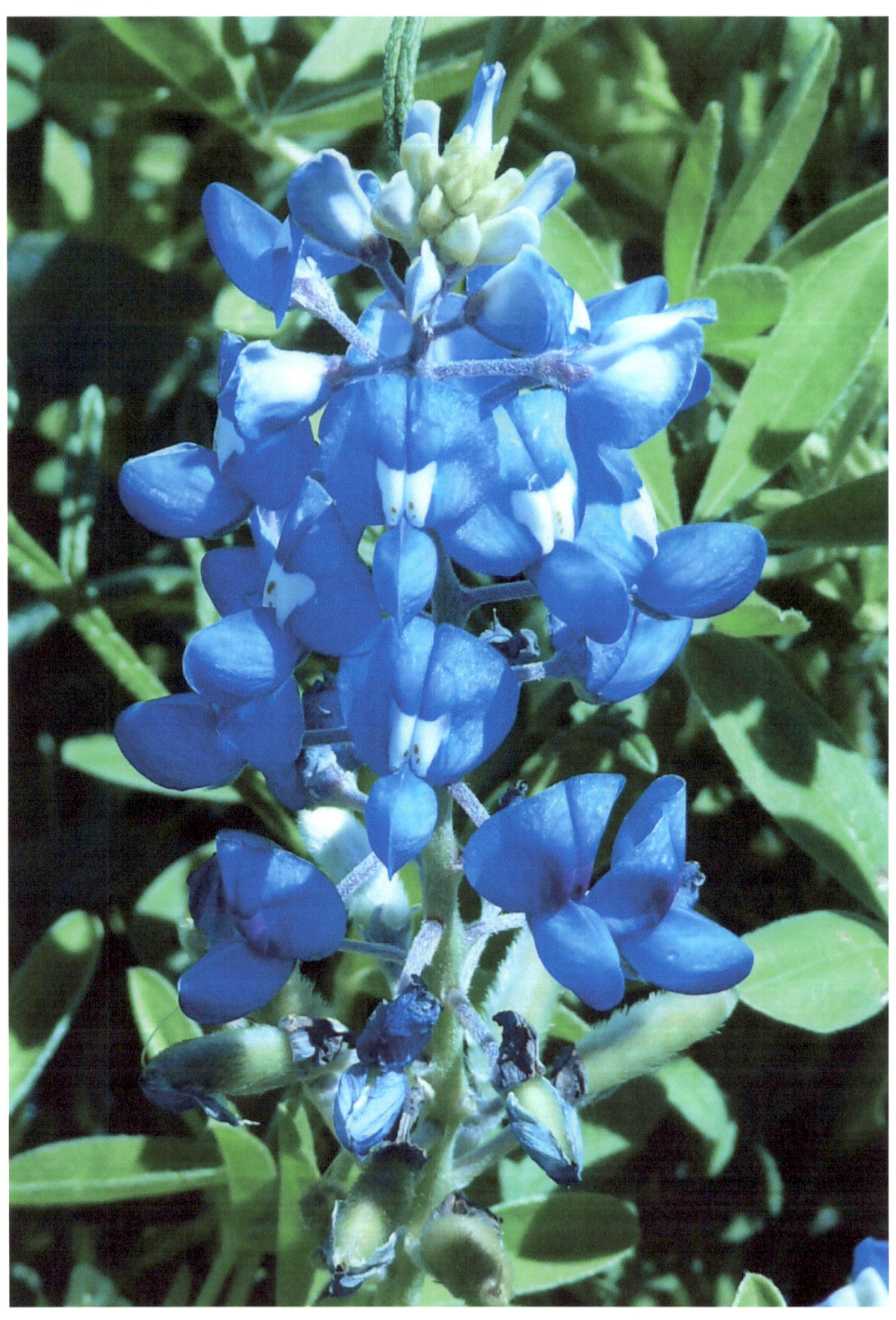

Bluebonnets at a park in San Antonio, Texas

Carousel Zebra

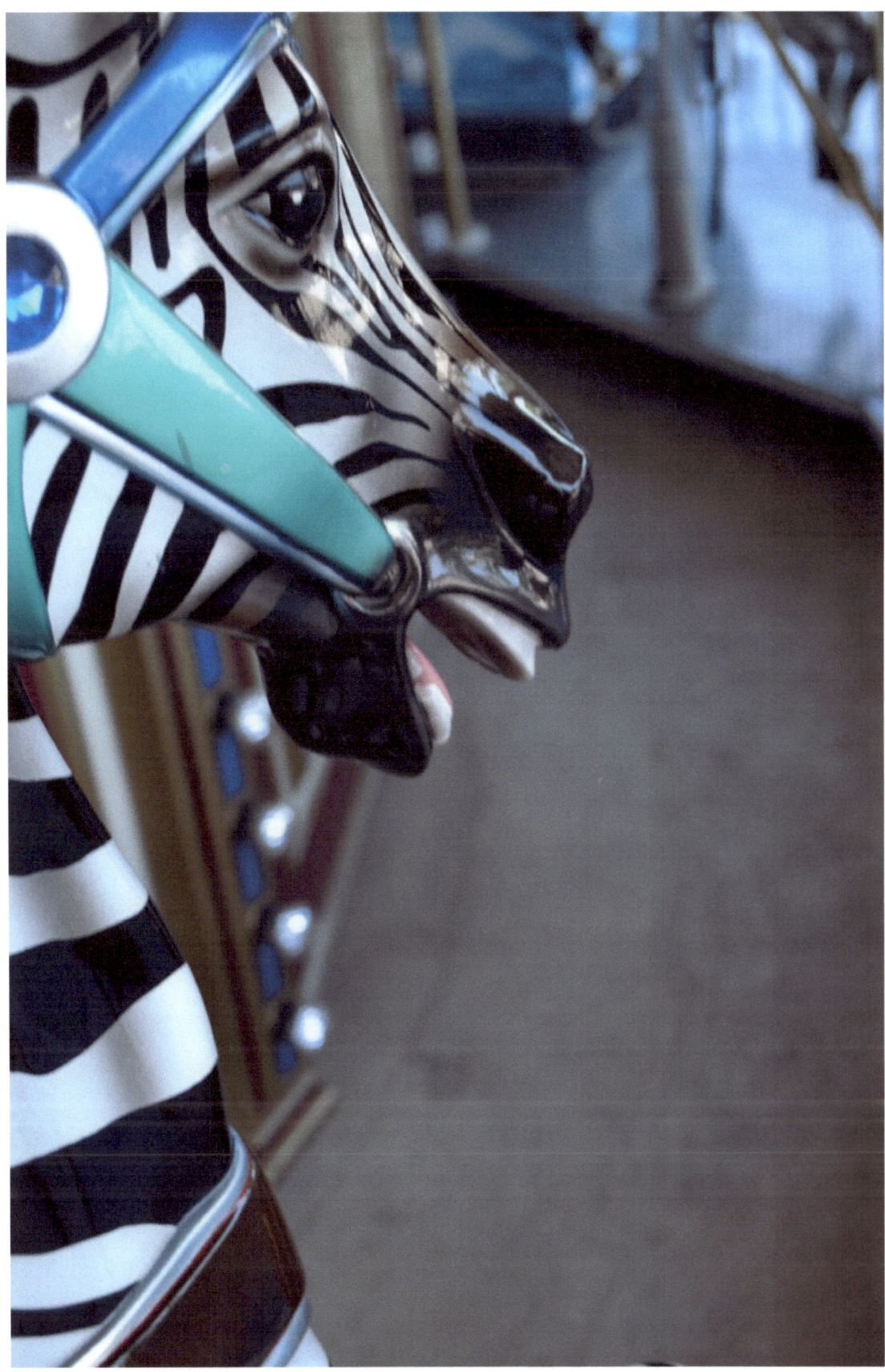

Zebra on the carousel at "Morgan's Wonderland" in San Antonio, Texas

Spurs Coyote

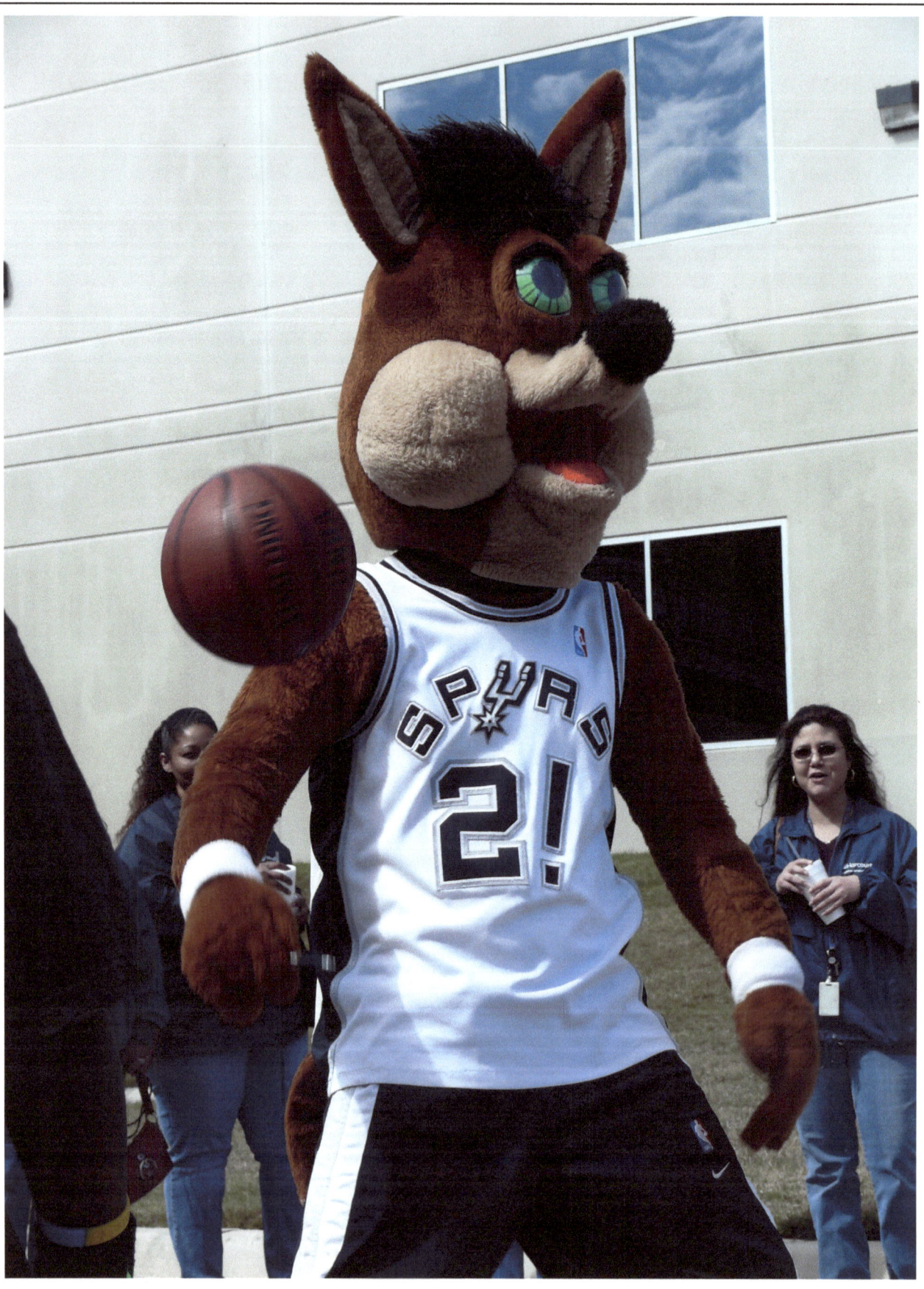

The Spurs Coyote entertains employees during a visit to Harcourt Assessment in San Antonio, Texas

Earl Abel's

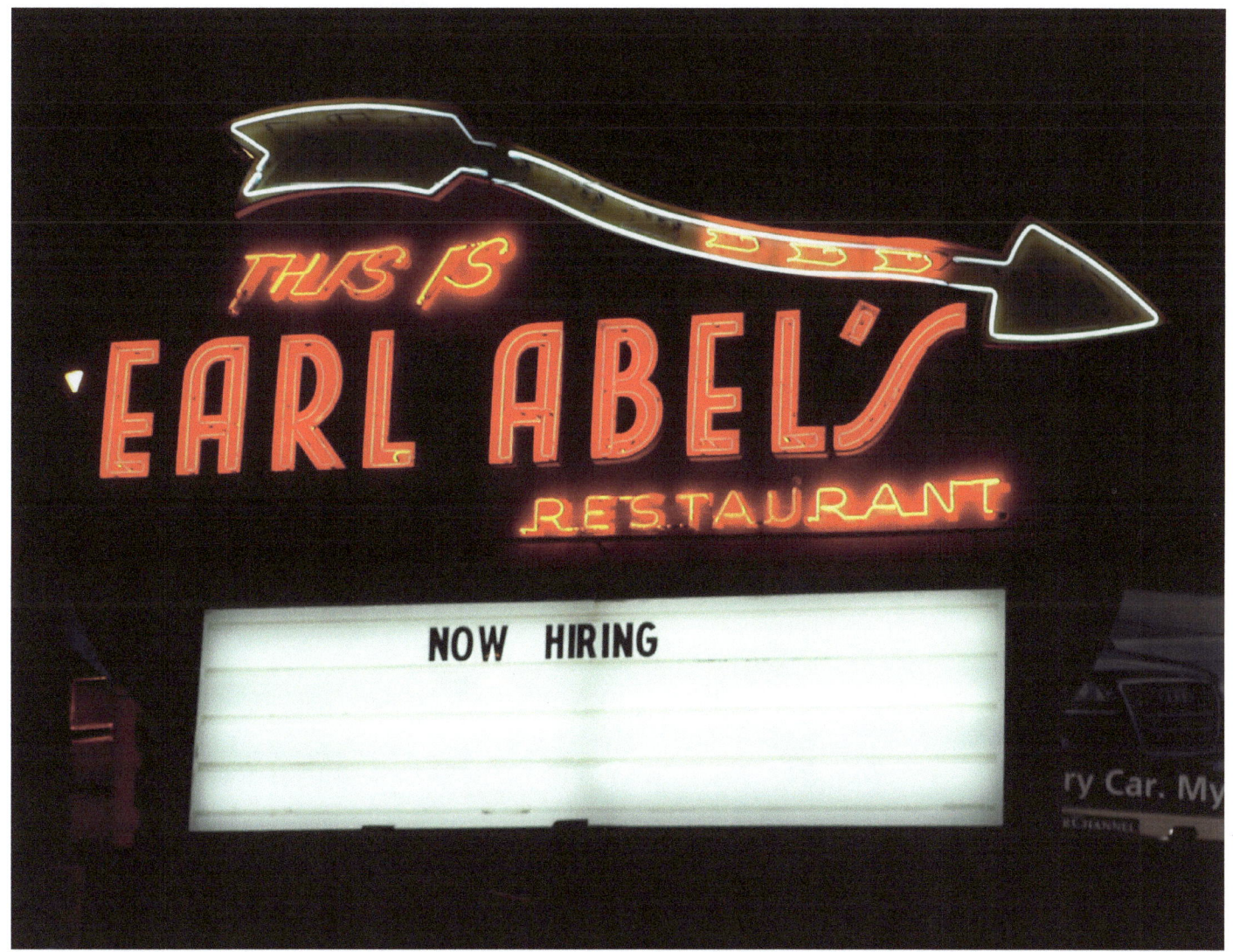

Earl Abel's sign on Broadway in San Antonio, Texas

Windmill

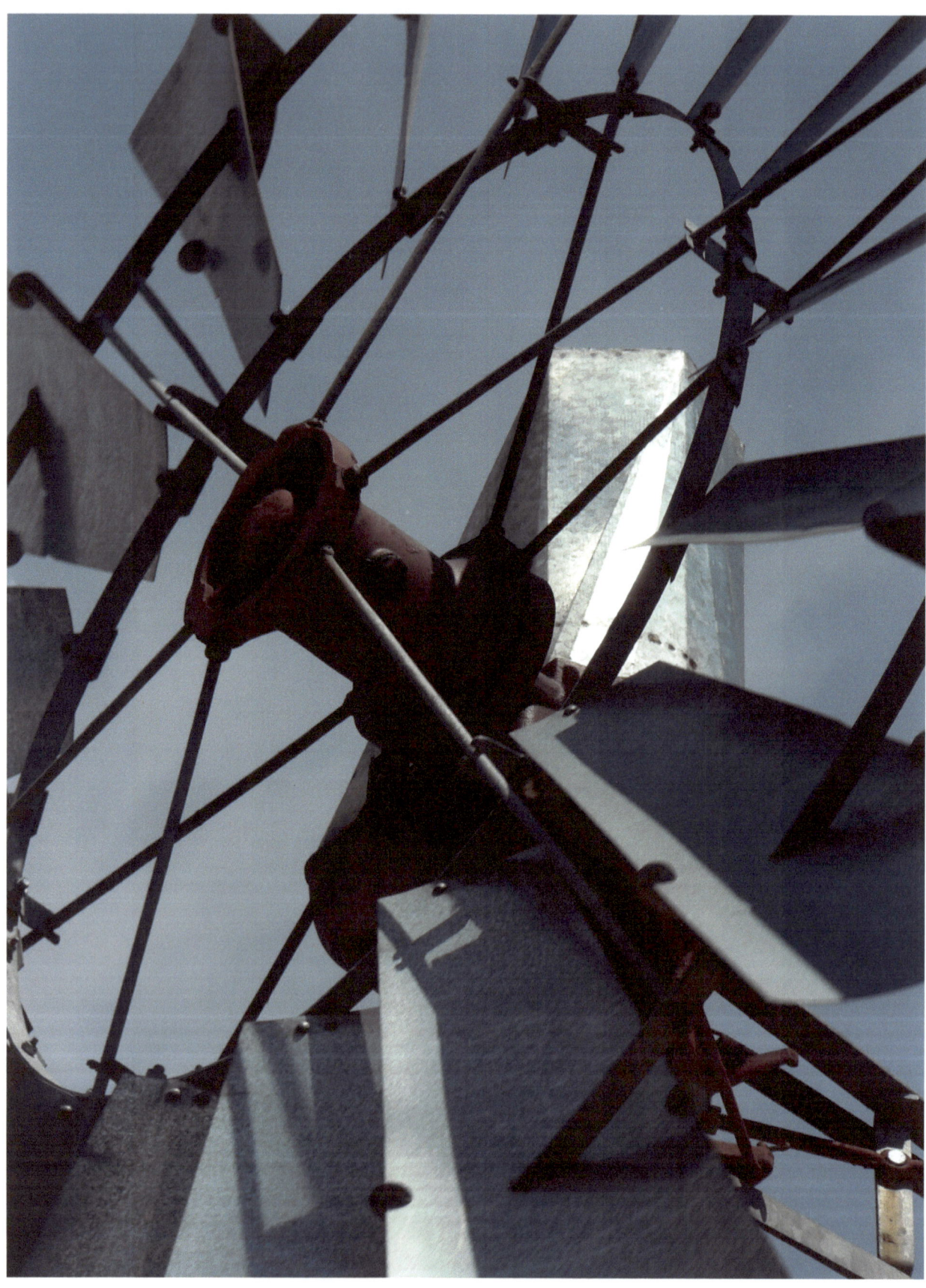

Close-up view of a windmill at Enchanted Springs near Boerne, Texas

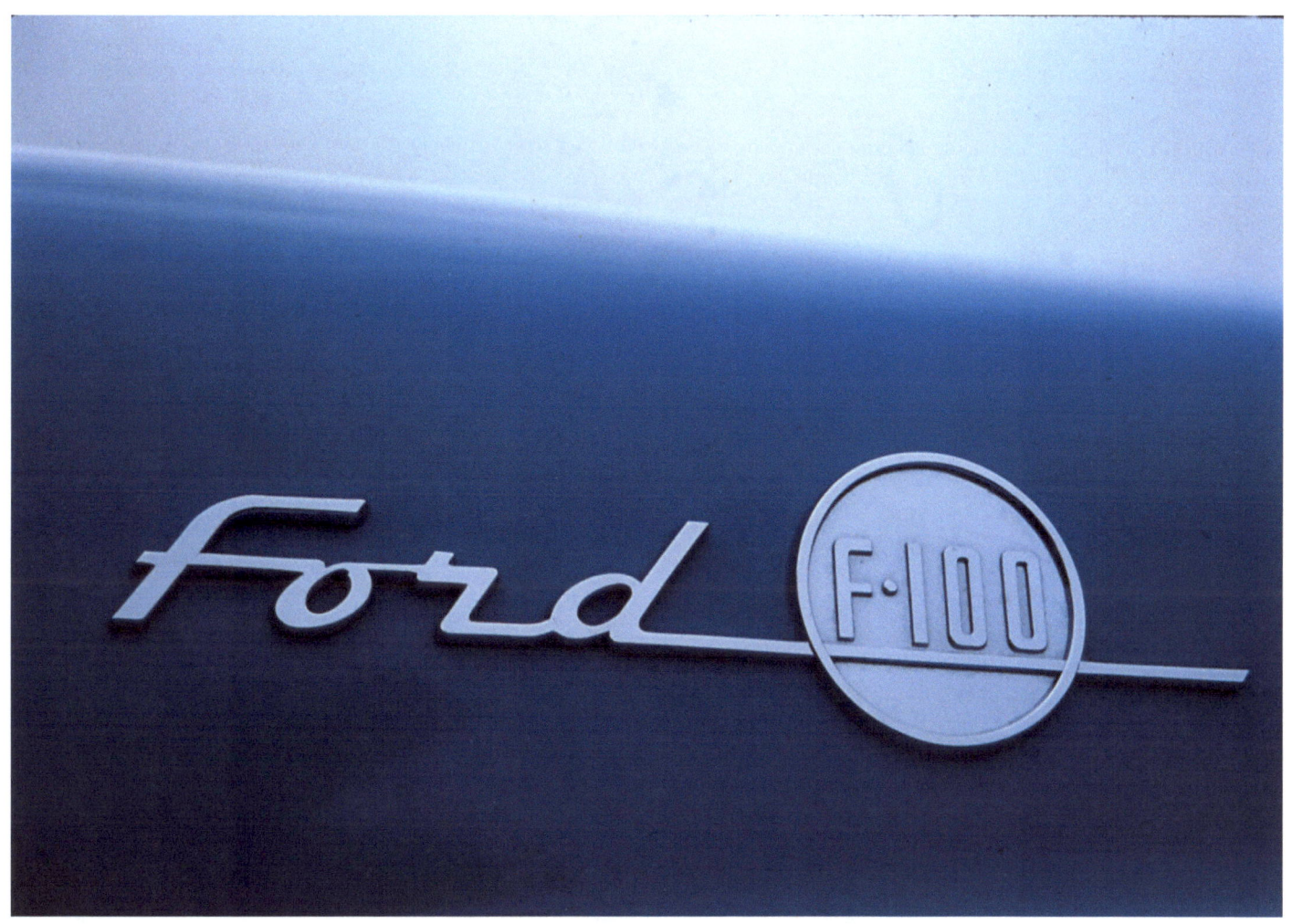

Ford F-100 logo at a car show

Frog

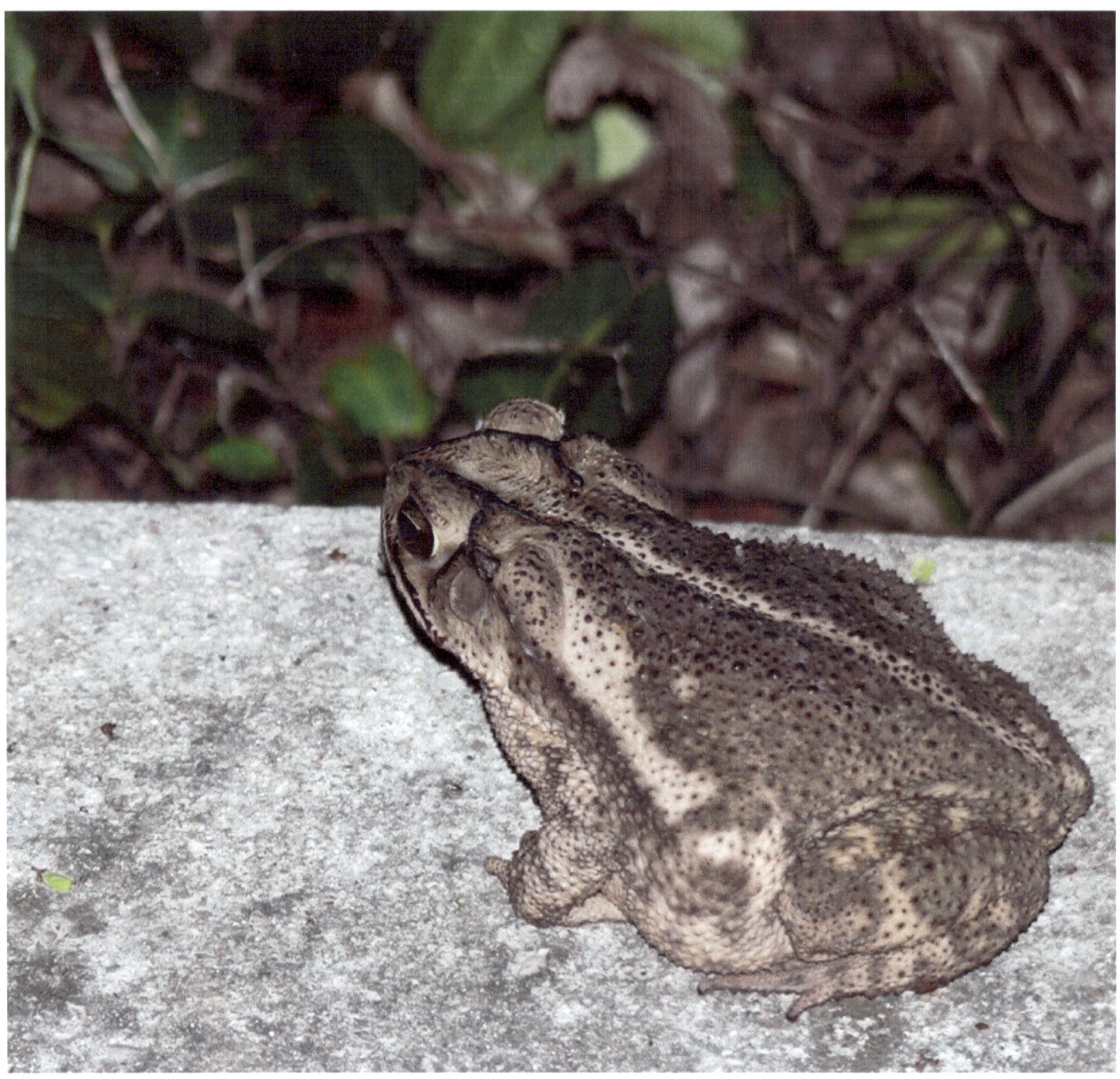

Frog on a sidewalk at an apartment complex in San Antonio, Texas

Gonzales Courthouse

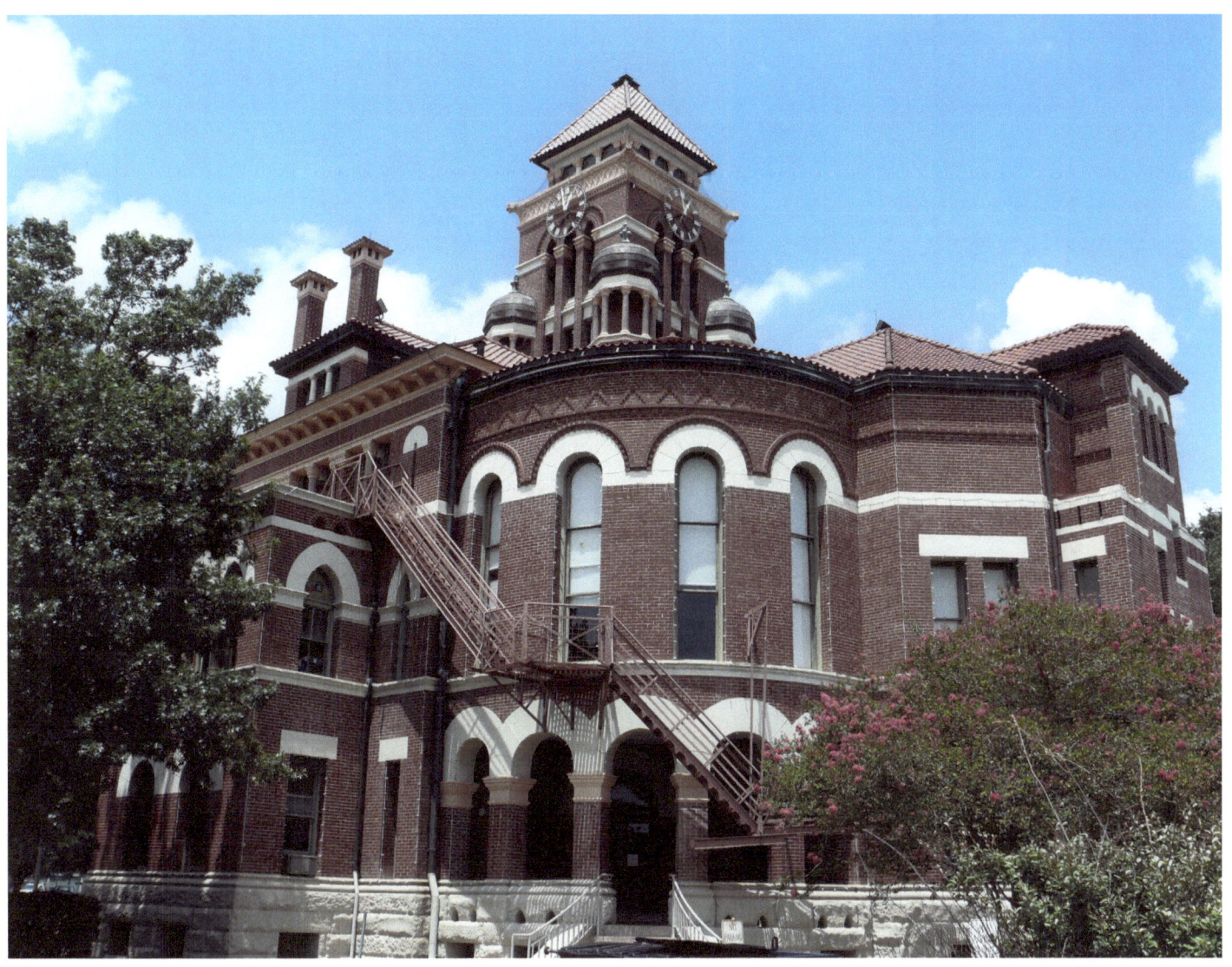

Gonzales County Courthouse in Gonzales, Texas

Ice Storm #1

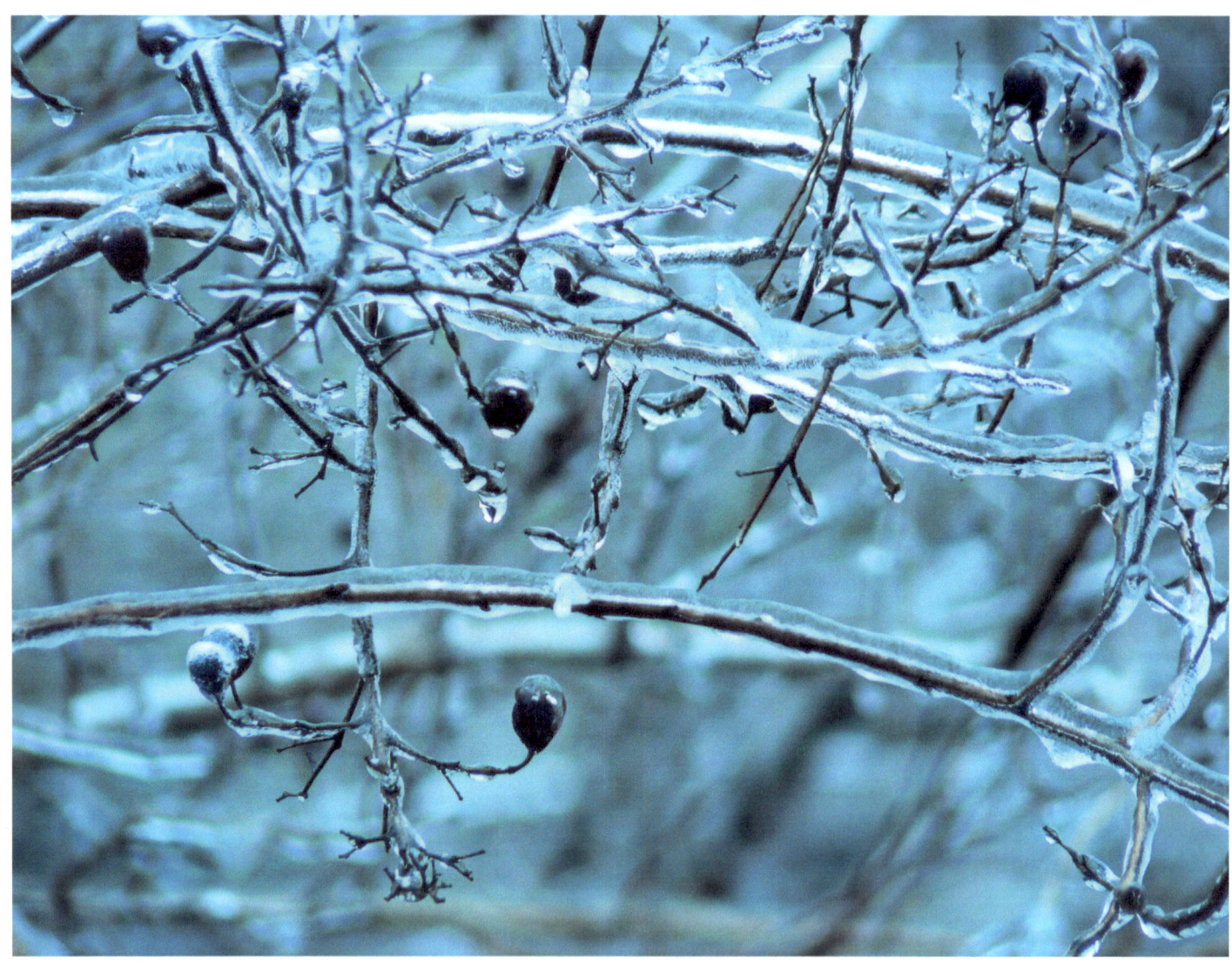

Ice on a tree after an ice storm in January 2007 in San Antonio, Texas

Ice Storm #2

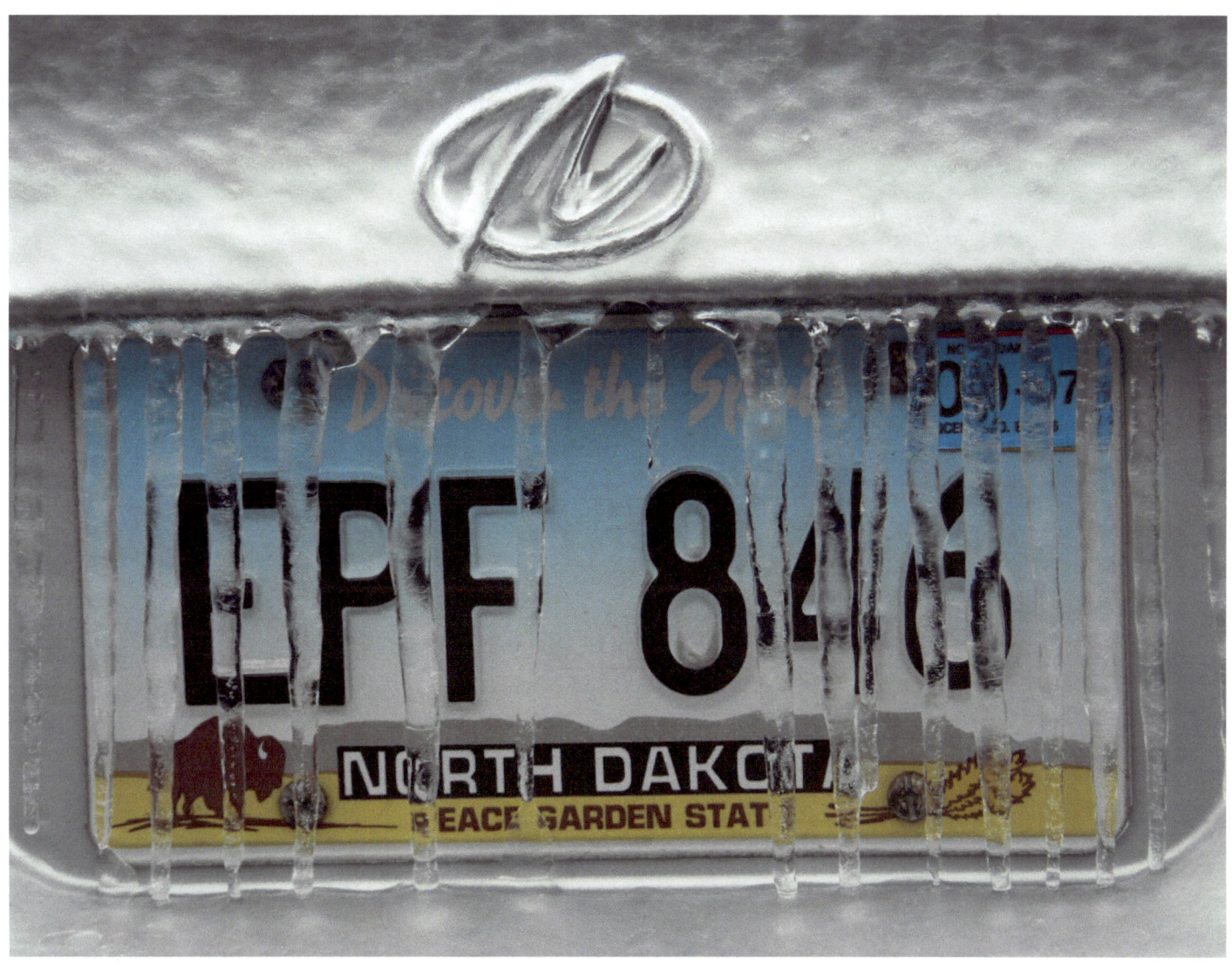

Ice on a car after an ice storm in January 2007 in San Antonio, Texas

Lavaca County Courthouse

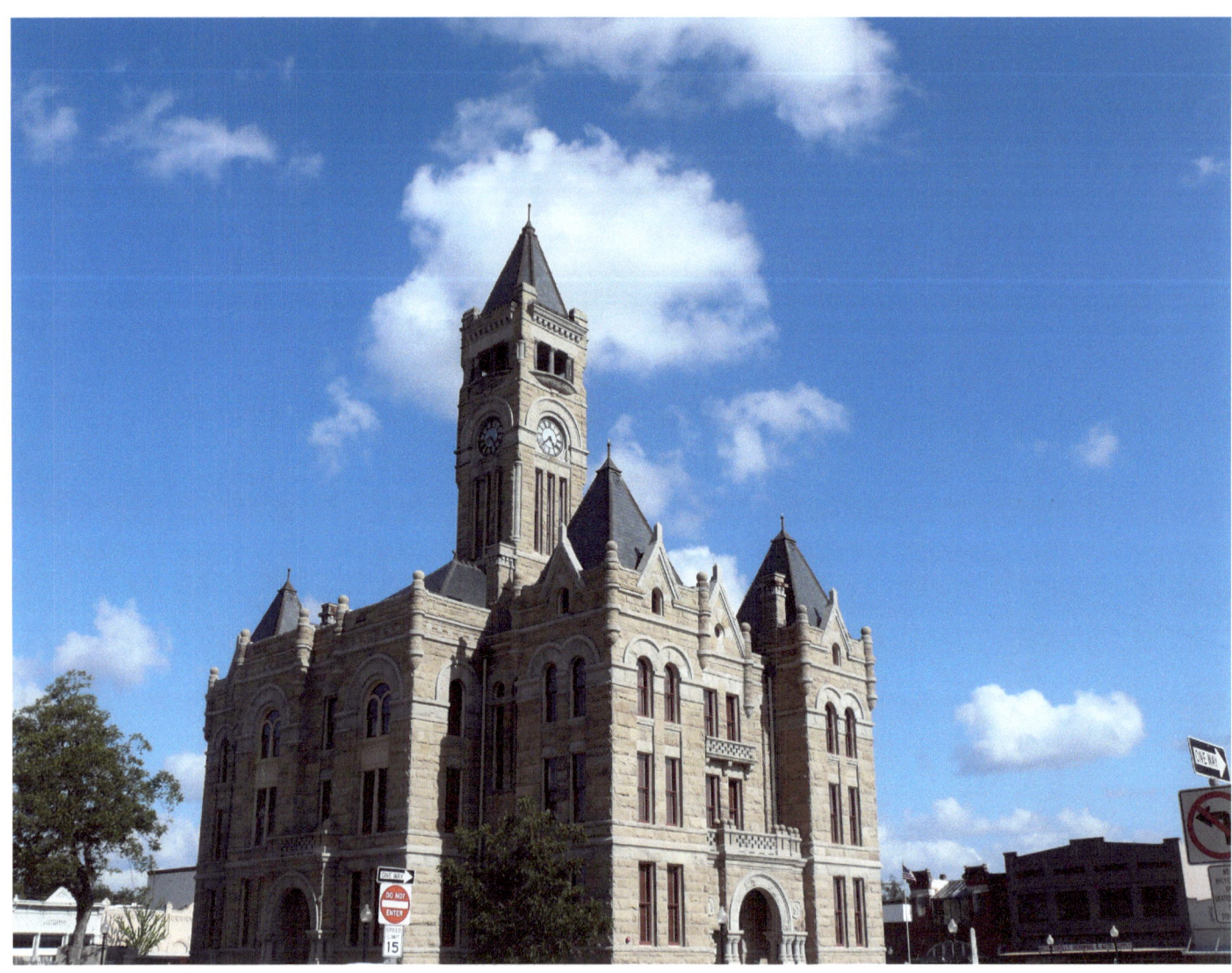

Lavaca County Courthouse in Hallettsville, Texas

Lourdes Grotto Statue

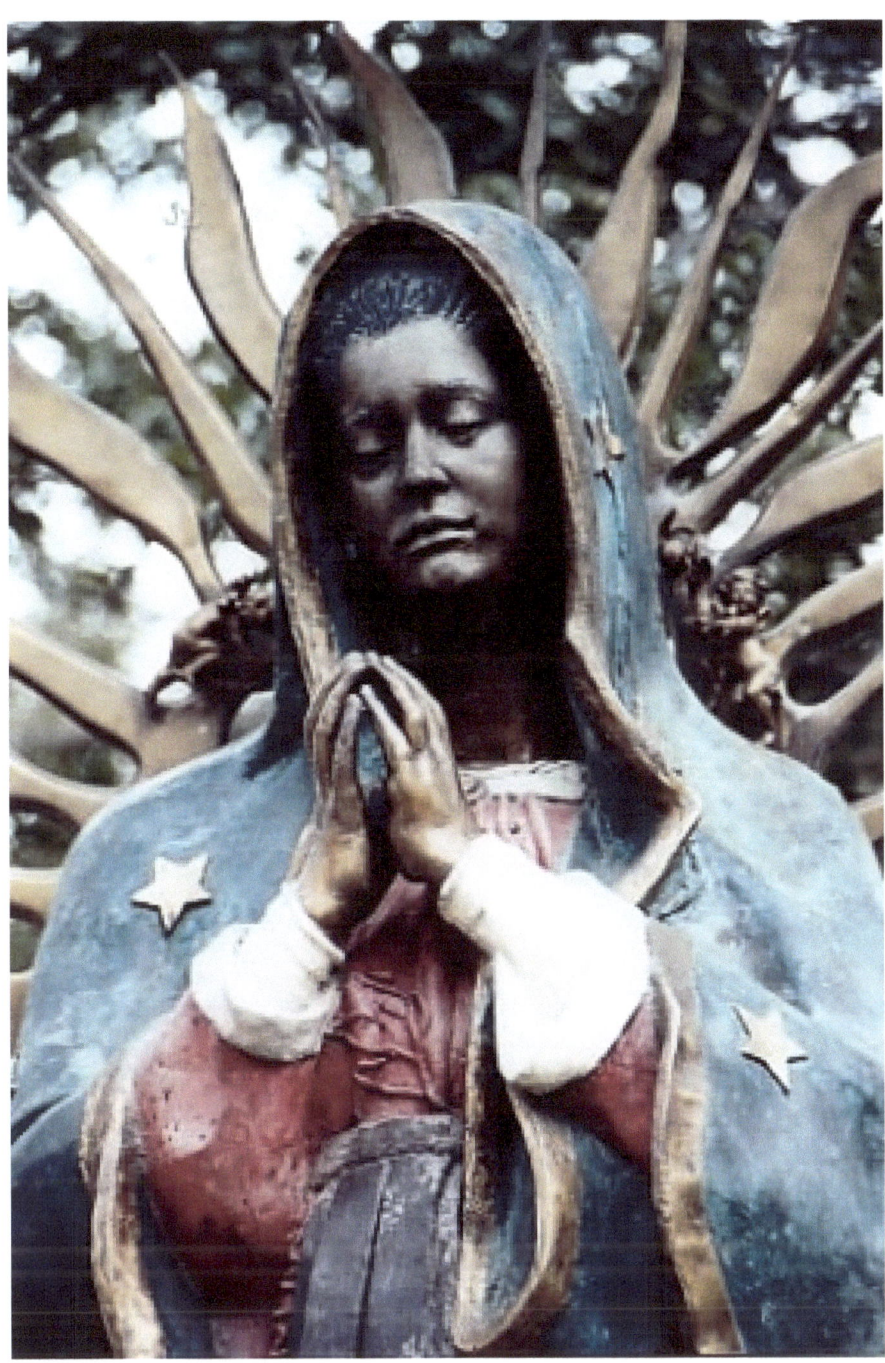

Statue at Lourdes Grotto in San Antonio, Texas

Luling Railroad Tracks

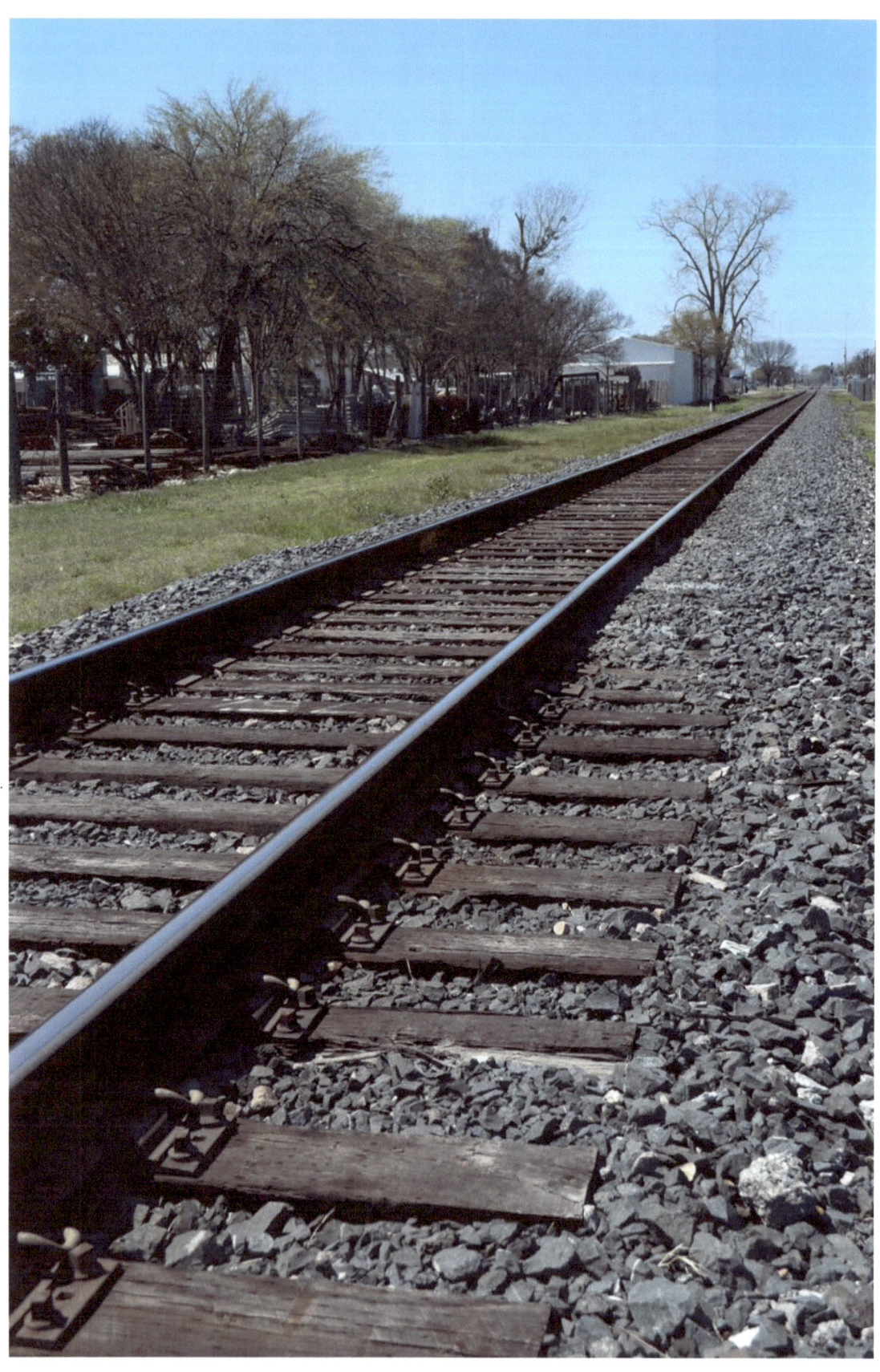

Railroad Tracks in Luling, Texas

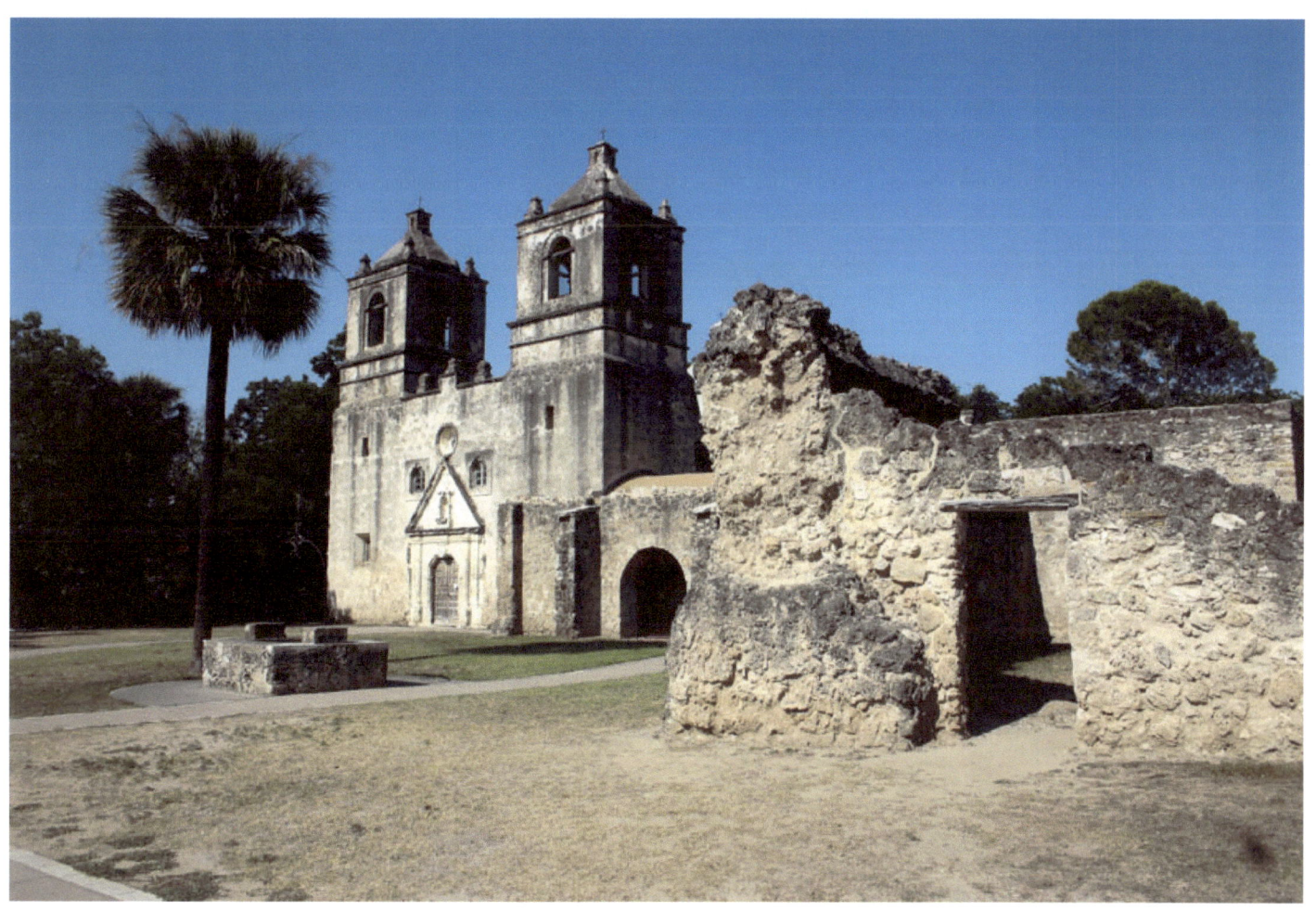

Mission Concepcion in San Antonio, Texas

St. Joseph's Church

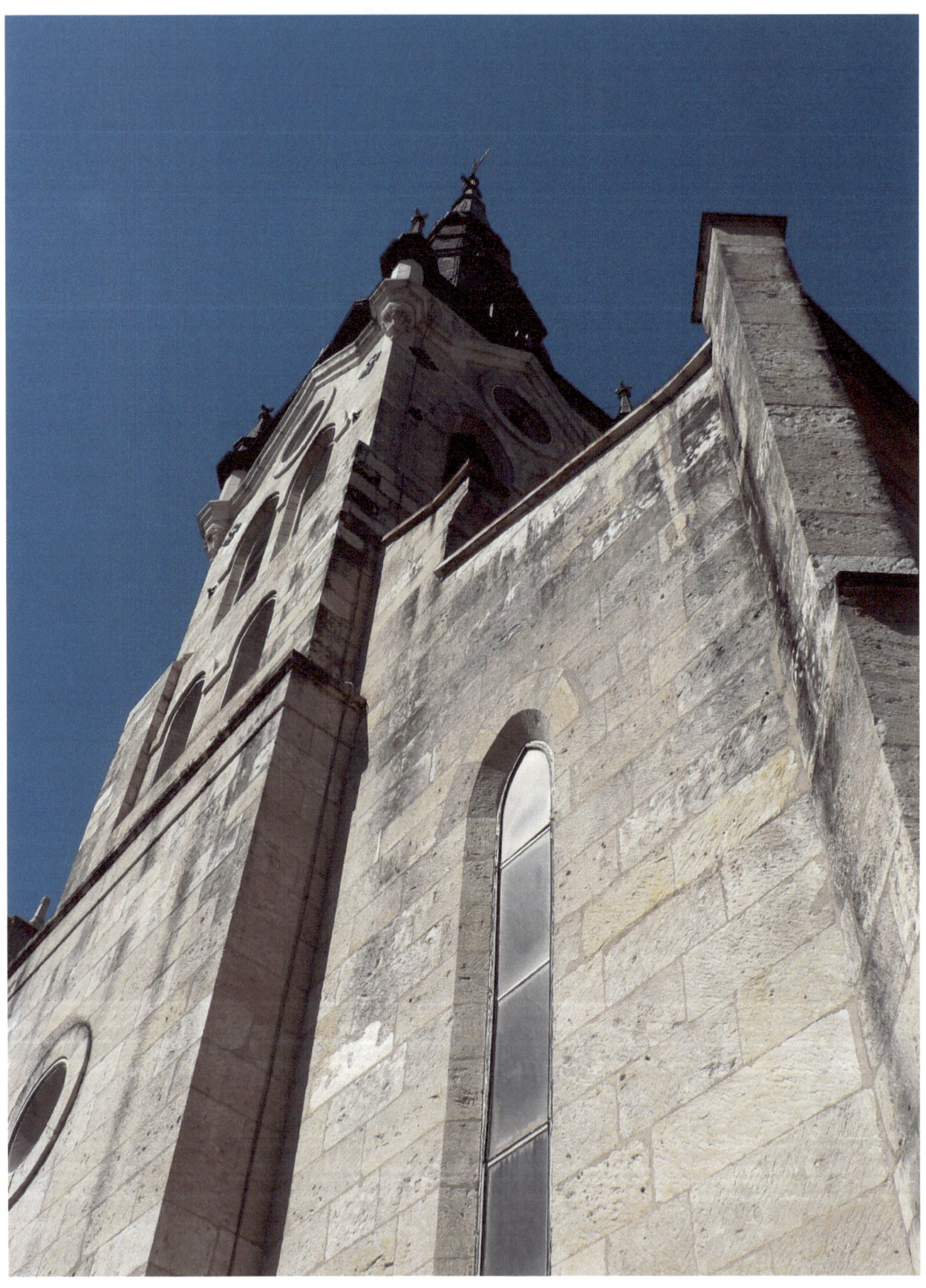

St. Joseph's Church in downtown San Antonio, Texas

Stingray

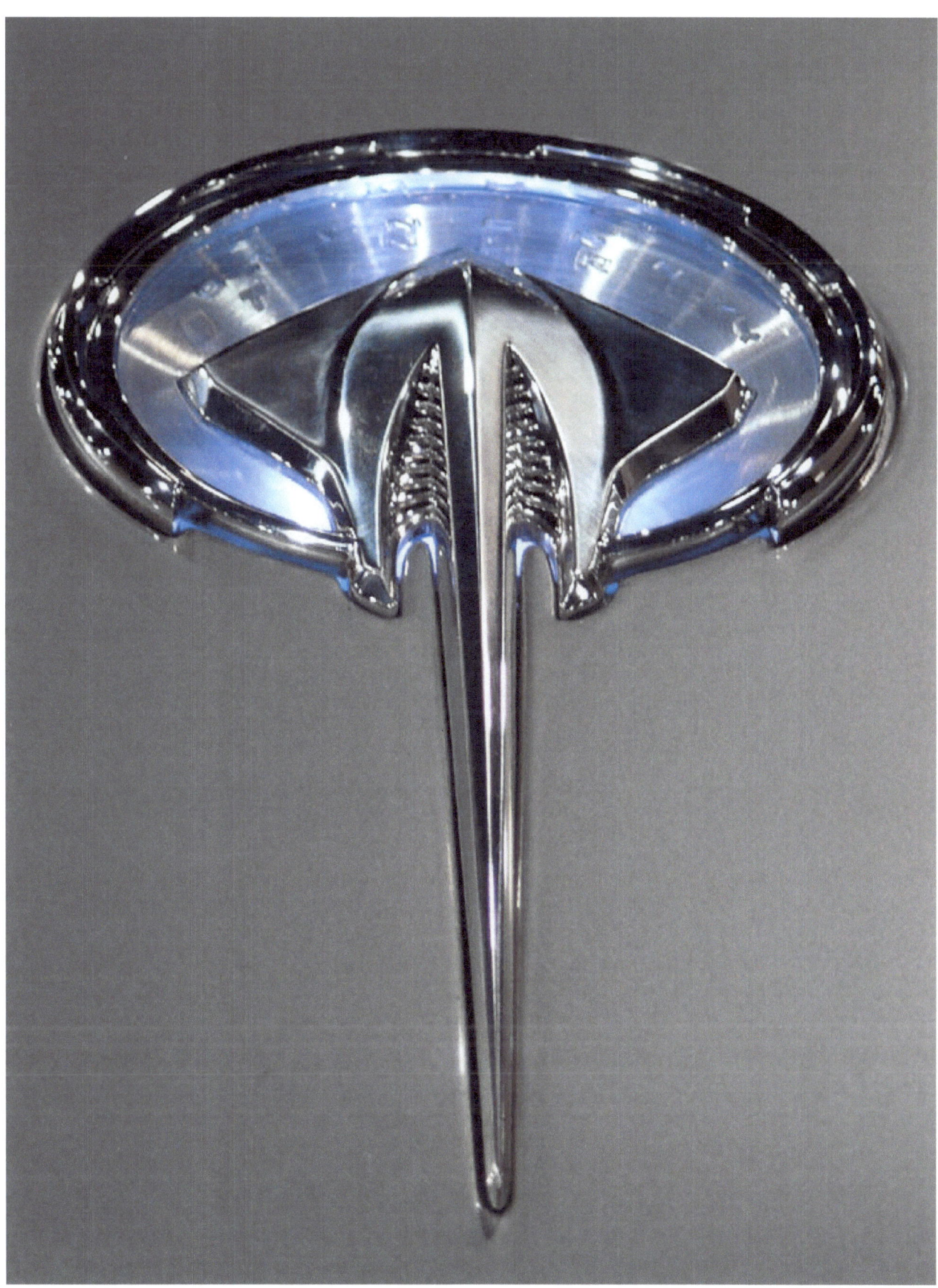

Stingray logo at a car show

Tower Life Building

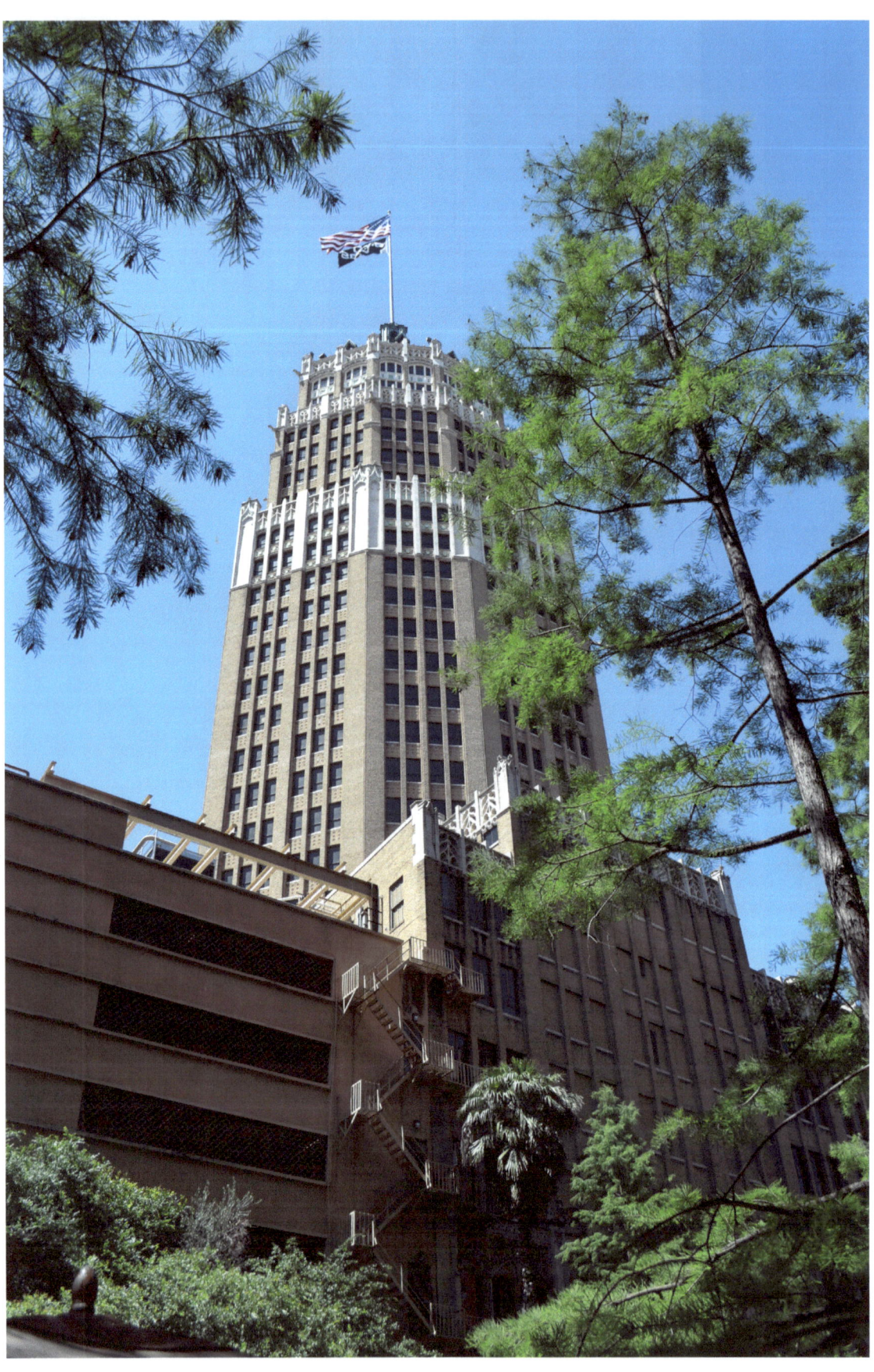

Tower Life Building in San Antonio, Texas

Tower Silhouette

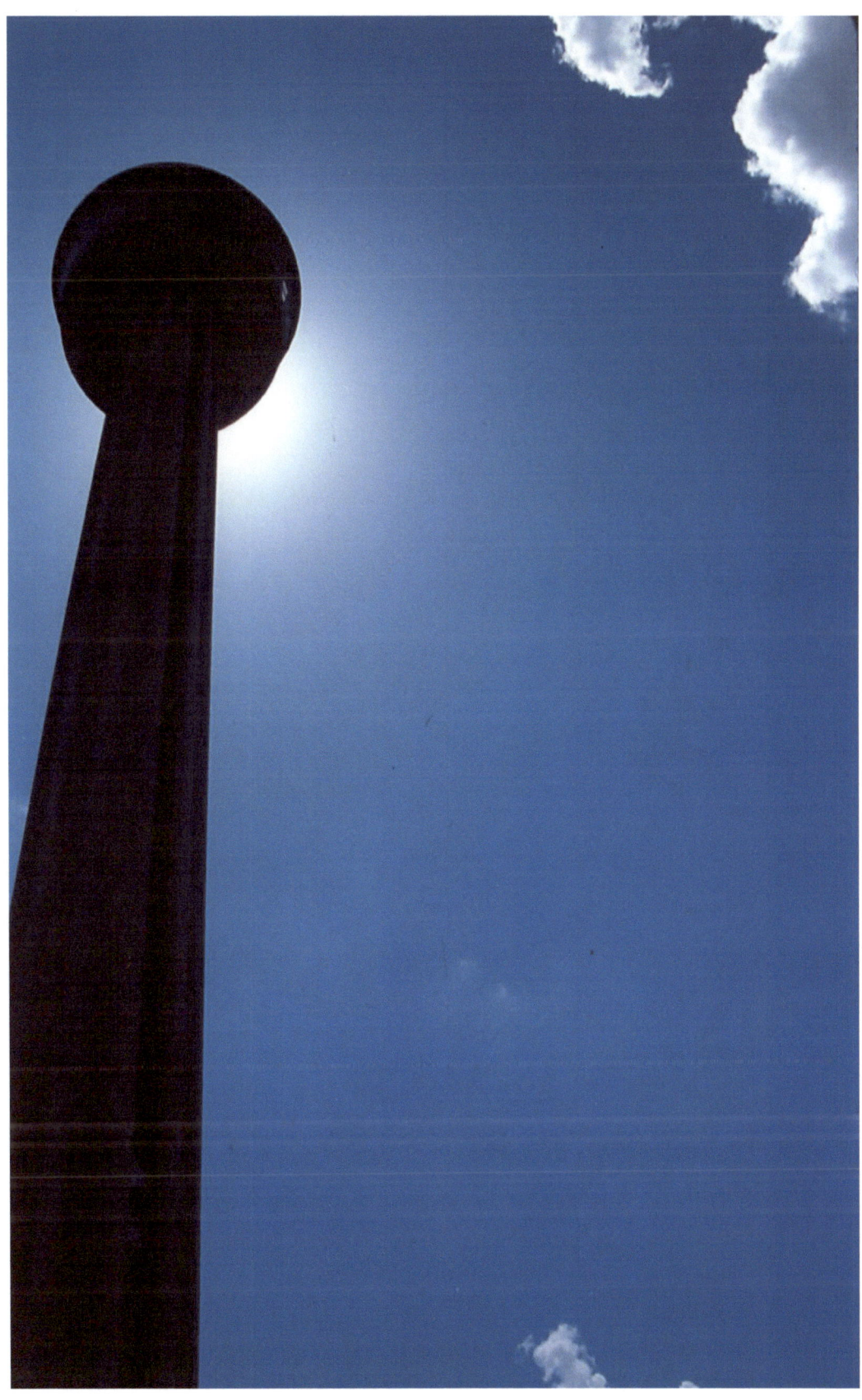

Silhouette of the Tower of the Americas in San Antonio, Texas

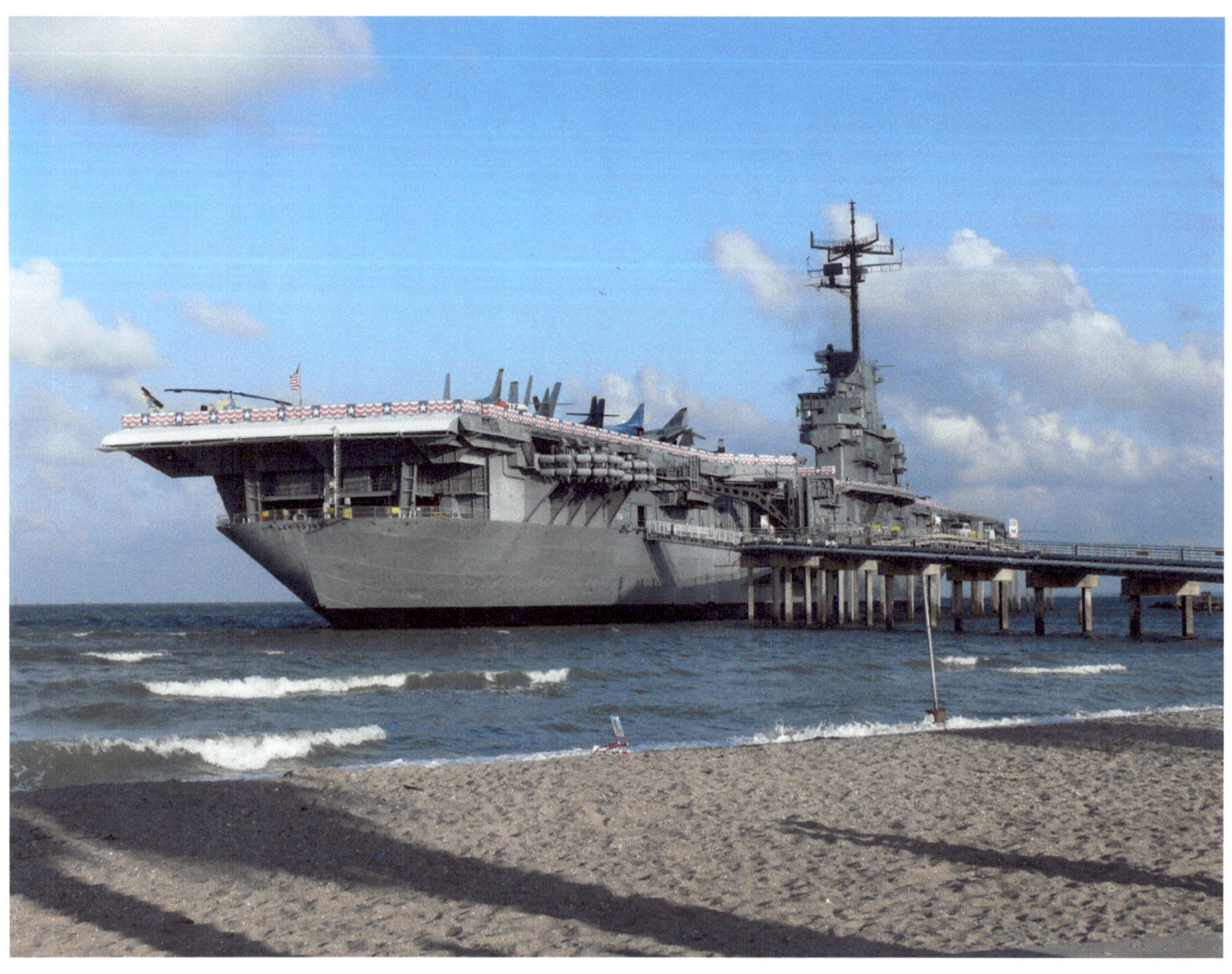

The USS Lexington in Corpus Christi, Texas in May 2012

The
End!

My photos are also online at:

http://www.texasphotodude.com/

Other books by Adam Kincher:

Photography:

A Look Through My Lens: Photos by Adam Kincher: http://
www.amazon.com/Look-Through-My-Lens-Kincher/dp/1492323276/
ref=sr_1_1?ie=UTF8&qid=1404706250&sr=8-1&keywords=adam+kincher
(September 2013)

Comics:

The Big Book of Mr. Small: http://www.amazon.com/The-Big-Book-Mr-
Small/dp/149231773X/ref=sr_1_1?ie=UTF8&qid=1378692268&sr=8-
1&keywords=adam+kincher (September 2013)

The 2nd Big Book of Mr. Small: http://www.amazon.com/The-2nd-Big-Book
-Small/dp/1500451142/ref=sr_1_2?ie=UTF8&qid=1405265302&sr=8-
2&keywords=adam+kincher (July 2014)

www.ingramcontent.com/pod-product-compliance
Lightning Source LLC
Chambersburg PA
CBHW040754200526
45159CB00025B/2091